Here I Am

Faith Stories of Korean American Clergywomen

Edited by Grace Ji-Sun Kim

Foreword by Neal D. Presa

—

To all the courageous Korean American women
who dared to follow their call
trusting in our living God.

—

Here I Am: Faith Stories of Korean American Clergywomen

Interior design by Crystal Devine.
Cover design by Wendy Ronga, Hampton Design Group.

Library of Congress Cataloging-in-Publication data

Here I am : faith stories of Korean American clergywomen / Grace Ji-Sun Kim, editor ; foreword by Neal Presa. -- First [edition].
pages cm
ISBN 978-0-8170-1763-7 (pbk. : alk. paper) 1. Women clergy. 2. Korean American women. 3. Women in church work. I. Kim, Grace Ji-Sun, 1969- editor.
BV676.H475 2015
277.3'083082--dc23
2015004054

Printed in the U.S.A.

First printing, 2015.

Contents

PART III: Korean American Sermons

Foreword

Christianity is a faith tradition of many stories. The Holy Scripture is an anthology of the stories of people whom the living God has encountered and whose lives are affected by this encounter. The written medium, now available on e-readers, tablets, and smartphones, came to us as sacred stories that were told, retold, and ritualized in family hearths, the tabernacle, the first and second temples, the synagogue, and the house church. The living faith takes root in particular contexts, in the idioms and idiosyncrasies of specific cultures, whether in the form of bread and wine or rice and tea. The living faith of God in Christ through the Holy Spirit *stories*[1] us.

It has always been that way: the living, breathing story of the faith *stories* a people. *Story* as a verbed noun has two functions: a **constitutive** and a **unitive** function. In its **constitutive** function, the Judeo-Christian faith informs and shapes our contextual realities, births a community called "Christian," and places as the identifying marker at the center and circumference of such a community that herein are followers of a man called Jesus the Christ. As a constituting action, story *stories* the acts of that community, so breaking a piece of bread is not merely splitting a loaf, but it is partaking in the Communion of our Lord's body; being immersed in water is not merely about liquid on someone's head, but it is being initiated into the death and resurrection of our Lord.

But *story* as a verbed noun also has a **unitive** function. Jewish theology reminds us that remembering is not merely about cognitive memory (Greek *anamnesis*). Remembering is about "re-membering," being connected to the life and faith of God's people in every time and in all places. God unites us to Sarah, to Moses, to Esther, to Mary Magdalene, to Mother Teresa, to Martin Luther King Jr. The sacred stories of the faith told and retold, from paper pages through modern technology and through verbal and ritualized forms, become our stories; we participate in them and they in us, all of us in the stories of every generation. In this way, we can say quite confidently, "I was at the Red Sea. I was at the Jordan River."[2]

As a Filipino American married to a Korean American (which means our two sons are "Korinos" or "Filo-reans"!), I was born, raised, and married into families that were storied. Both of our families and extended families in the Philippines, Guam, Korea, and the United States come from a *storied* past, a living story in the present, and a *story-ing* future. That is the way it is in Asian American cultures: we love stories—telling them, hearing them, again and again.

As Asian American Christians, story becomes all the more important because there is so much more to tell. There is more to internalize and metabolize in the fibers and sinews of our communities. Those of us who are Asian Americans know at some level of the deep struggles, pain, and hardship of our grandparents and parents, and what living in the United States meant for them and for the families they raised. That storied past also reveals how Christianity in the Asian and Asian American expressions of living the faith provided both a place of community and/or the perpetuation of struggle needing redemption.

Yet, within the vastness of the stories of the faith and the *storying* of communities (in both their constitutive and unitive aspects), there remains a gap; it's a gap of an essential perspective on the faith—that from women who are ordained ministers who are Korean American.

In many settings of the church and in its councils at all levels, I have seen and heard of the great giftedness of Korean American clergywomen colleagues and have been blessed tremendously by their preaching, pastoral care, and leadership; my ministry and life, as with so many others, have been enriched by them. Yet, in far too many settings of the church and its councils, I have also seen and heard the church silencing their daughters of the faith, disregarding their witness, stifling their passion, questioning their callings, or using them to advance some partisan agenda.

I do not pretend to know myself the struggles of my Korean American sisters in Christ and colleagues in the pastoral ministry; theirs is a story that needs to be told, because whenever stories of the faith are presented, they constitute and reconstitute, unite and reunite the communities of faith. The stories of Korean American clergywomen need to be told by *them*, on *their* terms, in *their* way. What this present volume brings to the church is a treasury of gifts, in response to which we must listen, receive, rejoice, be critiqued, laugh, and cry. In other words, their stories become our stories while at the same time remaining their own; it is a mutual participation in their stories as part of the faith while simultaneously being their own distinct, unique perspective on life and faith to which we are invited to see and discern our common faith and our distinct humanities.

The Reverend Dr. Grace Ji-Sun Kim and her fellow contributing writers are faithful in their ministries and in the telling of their personal and family narratives. *Here I Am: Faith Stories of Korean American Clergywomen* brings into our conscience stories of struggles, vocations, identities, and spiritualities in church communities that provided formation but also perpetuated oppression toward the very women who sought to answer God's call to serve as ministers in their Korean American communities or in the wider church.

But the power of their narratives does not merely remain with the telling, as necessary and critical as that is. Their narratives call the church—in its Korean/Korean American, Asian/Asian American, and Anglo privileged expressions—to come to terms with what stories of the faith are being told, how such stories are being told, and how those stories are being lived in every generation. Theirs is a powerful truth telling to what the church needs to hear and with what it needs to struggle. In valuable ways, Kim and the contributors to this important volume are prophets among us—calling all storytellers of the faith to be reconstituted and reunited to every aspect of our storied faith, especially those stories that have been forgotten, those that have been neglected, and those that have been taken for granted. This is a call to be more faithful and honest.

In an earlier book called *Growing Healthy Asian American Churches*,[3] Peter Cha and his coeditors use the notion of household as the organizing framework to speak of churches as households of grace and truth, hospitable communities of mercy and justice, places that care about gender relations and intergenerational giftedness. May *Here I Am* catalyze spaces in church and society to become sacred arenas of grace and truth, and holy forums where stories of mercy and justice abound and are told, welcomed, and generously received.

Neal D. Presa
Rancho Santa Fe, CA
3rd Week in Pentecost 2014

NOTES

1. In this foreword, I employ "verbing," an etymological process in grammar studies of using one part of speech for another, in this case using a noun—story—as a verb, a process known more generally as *anthimeria*.

2. Walter Brueggeman coined the term "imaginative remembering" to describe the "traditioning" process of canonization and transmission of textualized stories of the faith as it emerged dynamically through the interplay of historical, cultural, ideological, political, and religious forces in the ancient Near East. I borrow his *verbing* of tradition to *traditioning* to speak of the Christian faith stories as *storying* us. In both senses—traditioning and storying—the point is amplified that our faith as told, retold, canonized, and textualized is not archived and curated; rather it lives and breathes as the living God speaks in and through the stories to living, breathing human beings and communities. See Brueggeman's *An Introduction to the Old Testament: The Canon and Christian Imagination* (Louisville: Westminster John Knox Press, 2003).

3. Peter Cha, S. Steve Kang, and Helen Lee, eds., *Growing Healthy Asian American Churches: Ministry Insights from Groundbreaking Congregations* (Downers Grove, IL: IVP Books, 2006).

Acknowledgments

This book, *Here I Am: Faith Stories of Korean American Clergywomen*, emerged with the help of many people and communities. First among them is the Korean American Presbyterian Clergywomen (KAPCW), an organization established in 1991. The Korean American Presbyterian Clergywomen had long desired to commemorate its twenty-fifth anniversary with a publication that contained stories of Korean American women as they journeyed through the various landscapes of ministry. The project began to take form thanks to the 2013–14 Board of Directors under the leadership of Eun Joo Kim, president of the board. The 2013–14 board members—Mickie Choi, Soon Hee Earm, Na Young Ha, Michelle Hwang, Yena K. Hwang, Grace Ji-Sun Kim, Jung Sook Kim, Joann Haejong Lee, Unzu Lee, Ann Rhee Menzie, Irene Pak, Heidi Park, Marion Park, and Angela Ryo—shepherded this book throughout its journey. The Korean American Presbyterian Clergywomen's Board of Directors, both past and present, have a deep appreciation for the Korean American women engaged in ministry and are invested in the KAPCW's future, growth, and legacy. This publication is a great way to celebrate this organization and its meaningful work.

There are many individual people to thank. These include the senior founding members of the Korean American Presbyterian Clergywomen's group: Jean Kim, Ann Rhee-Menzie, Unzu Lee, Mickie Choi, Marion Park, and Mary Paik, who saw the need for such a group and initiated and wisely shepherded us for the past twenty-five years. They have worked tirelessly for the larger church and made sacrifices to pave the way for the next generation of Korean clergywomen. I also want to thank each contributor in this volume for her deep theological insights, her personal devotion to the church, and her willingness to share her own vulnerability. It took courage, dedication, vision, and diligence to write these narratives in the midst of busy lives, ministries, childbirth, mothering, and taking care of loved ones. I am grateful for the dedication and writing of these women.

I am grateful also to the good people at Judson Press who took a risk in publishing the stories of Korean American clergywomen. Warm thanks to Rebecca Irwin-Diehl for working with me on so many levels to ensure the timely publication of this book. Also many thanks go to Lisa Blair and Linda Johnson-LeBlanc for all their assistance with the manuscript, and particularly for setting up the Pubslush campaign to help fund the book.

This book is put together with the help of generous donors, among them many family members and friends. I would like to acknowledge the generosity of those who contributed more than one hundred and fifty dollars: Margaret Aymer Oget, Molly Casteel, David Rue, Cynthia Holder Rich, Sung Yeon Choimorrow, Jeannie Kim, Mark Koenig, Mickie Choi, Suk Jong Lee, Anne Rhee-Menzie, Joseph Ahn, and the Korean American Presbyterian Clergywomen (KAPCW). Your generous donations helped us to realize our dream.

Two other very important people generously invested their time, energy, and gifts to help bring this book to publication. First, I am deeply indebted to Irene Pak for her imaginative writing, critique, and editorial skills, which made these chapters more readable. Second, I am greatly appreciative of Yena K. Hwang, who helped to edit many of the pieces in this book and provided valuable insight and encouragement. Both Yena and Irene's dedication, thoughtfulness, time, energy, and gifts have made this writing project enjoyable, doable, and delightful. I am grateful for their unbounded support and assistance along the way.

I must thank my sister, Karen, and brother-in-law, Bruce, for always supporting me in my writing. I thank my husband, Perry Lee, for his endless patience and for doing more than his share of driving our kids to their extracurricular activities. I also thank my three children, Theodore, Elisabeth, and Joshua, for standing by me and for enthusiastically sharing with me the excitement of seeing a book emerge. Your constant love and joy help me in more ways than you know.

Introduction

GRACE JI-SUN KIM

The book emerged from a conversation during an annual Korean American Presbyterian Clergywomen's (KAPCW) conference at McCormick Theological Seminary in Chicago in 2008. Initially, we wanted to compile a book to celebrate the twentieth anniversary of our group. However, the excitement around a possible book died down soon after the conference, as everyone got busy with her own life and work. Then in 2013, the board members of KAPCW revisited and rekindled this desire to publish, this time for our twenty-fifth anniversary in 2016. With renewed excitement, I volunteered to edit the book.

It was a long journey to get to the finished project, and it had its share of anxiety, excitement, and fulfillment. We are pleased to offer you the result, a volume that describes some of the delights, struggles, and difficulties of being Korean American clergywomen—a specific group of Asian American women who were born in the United States to Korean (American) parents or who have immigrated from Korea. Their stories provide a window through which to get a glimpse of the trials and tribulation of doing ministry within the American context.

Background of Asian American Immigration

Asians have migrated worldwide, but many Asians chose to migrate specifically to the United States and Canada. During the height of the United States's westward expansion and the building of its economy in the nineteenth century and beyond, Asian labor became a commodity to be used and traded. The annexation of California in 1848 opened the floodgates for Asian labor and prompted the arrival of many Asians such as the Japanese (1880s), Filipinos (1900), Koreans (1903), and Indians (1907) in the United States. They first came to Hawaii. Between 1850 and 1920, more than three hundred thousand Asians settled in those islands.[1] Initially, many Koreans had not wanted to immigrate to the United States, but some missionaries persuaded members of their congregations to go to Hawaii, as it was considered a Christian land. As a result, an estimated 40 percent of the 7,000 emigrants who left Korea between December 1902 and May 1905 were Christian converts.[2]

While some Korean women's immigration to the United States was initiated by the women's desire for greater freedom, it was men intent on profit and exploitation who induced others to emigrate.[3] Many women were misinformed and had high expectations of life in the United States. They had left Korea to escape patriarchy and to seek freedom from family obligations, but they found themselves captives under harsh and difficult working situations here in the States. Many were not ready for the hardships of immigrant life, finding the amount and nature of the work demanded of them to be unbearable. However, once they arrived, they found it was difficult to return to Korea. These were the beginnings of Korean women's immigrant lives in the United States.

Out of such history, background, and context have emerged important reflections, narratives, and theology from Korean immigrant women's lives. The distinct voices of Korean American women who have struggled and persevered through their religious and theological journeys are important to hear and examine. Experiences of immigration, marginalization, racism, sexism, and adaptation of their bi-religious heritages mark their history. *Here I Am: Faith Stories of Korean*

American Clergywomen is a collection of theological reflections, essays, sermons, stories of faith, and poetry by Korean American women in ministry.

Overview of the Book

This book is divided into three sections: Theological Reflections, Korean American Theology, and Korean American Sermons. Each section attempts to bring to light some of the deepest and most personal concerns of Korean American women in ministry. The reflections are raw, personal, and profound. The book begins with a foreword by Rev. Dr. Neal D. Presa and closes with an epilogue by Rev. Laura Mariko Cheifetz. It also has a brief historical narrative of the Korean Clergywomen's group by Rev. Dr. Unzu Lee. This is the first book of its kind, and we are moved by how it turned out.

The first section, Theological Reflections, begins with a chapter entitled "The Passage toward Parenthood as Vocational Practice" by Rev. Mihee Kim-Kort. She describes the work involved in having and raising a family. Being in a full-time ordained ministry only increases those challenges. However, the balancing act can open up a way to shape one's ministry, identity, and passions. Kim-Kort looks at the importance of intentionally working through the logistics of caring for a family with a partner (if one is available), creating boundaries that are physical, spiritual, and emotional in healthy differentiation, as well as surrendering to the possibilities of God, who continues to cultivate us as clergy through our families.

Rev. Dr. Grace Ji-Sun Kim describes her experience of being treated as a foreigner in, "'Do You Speak English?' Racial Discrimination and Being the 'Perpetual Foreigner.'" Traditionally, foreigners have been viewed with suspicion and as a source of many problems. Connecting her own experience of being seen as "foreign" with the treatment of foreign women in the biblical book of Ezra, Kim describes feelings of pain and tension. Relating an encounter in which she was asked, "Do you speak English?" Kim wonders how many more times she—and her children—will be asked the same question. She asserts that our churches and society must find a way to attend together to the fact that bodies marked by "foreignness" are hurting. She urges a critical reevaluation of how racist systems of power and privilege mark and identify people as "foreign" or "other" in small, but persistent ways.

Rev. Dr. Christine J. Hong shares her personal reflection on her journey toward ordination as a young Korean American woman in "Go Somewhere Else." It includes her painful confrontation and experience of sexism within the Korean American church. Hong shares how she prevailed despite these difficulties and found love, peace, and victory.

Rev. Yena K. Hwang shares a personal experience of "The Transformative Power of Communion." Hwang reflects on an encounter that challenged her perspective on the LGBTQ community and how the in-breaking of the Holy Spirit led her to have a more open and inclusive understanding of the body of Christ.

The second section of the book, Korean American Theology, begins with Rev. Nayoung Ha describing "The Urgent Need for an Ethic of Resistance in Korea." In her examination of the issues around the controversial legislation of the Anti-Discrimination Act in Korea, Ha argues that children, multicultural families, LGBTQ people, and politically radical, leftwing people are the outcasts in Korean society. She argues that Korean Christians must resist the dominant Christ, described as "a white racist, homophobic, and a politically religious right Christ," in order to be in solidarity with the outcasts in Korea.

"Home Sweet Diaspora Home" by Dr. Aram Bae describes how the Korean American church has become a "second home" to many who feel displaced, marginalized, and subordinated in their adopted land. Playing a multifaceted role, the Korean American church has become a place to share Korean culture and identity with the next generation. However, despite such positive attributes, the Korean American church also has its problems, which stem chiefly from its Confucian heritage. Bae shares her struggles of accepting this church "home" that has nurtured and called her into ministry, yet also oppresses her as a woman.

Rev. Jean Kim reflects on her lifetime of ministry with the homeless in "Woman in Purple—Ministry in Purple." She chronicles her difficult immigrant life, plagued by misfortunes, the deaths of family members, and experiences of racism, which ultimately led her to ordained ministry. Her journey to minister to the homeless is an inspiring testimony that helps us to understand the call of Jesus to serve the least of them.

Rev. Dr. Mickie Choi reflects on her call to ministry in "Miracle Baby." Born in Seoul, Korea, to a family of educators five days after the Korean War broke out, Choi immigrated to the United States after graduating from a college founded by the first Presbyterian missionary. As a chemistry major, Choi's American dream was to become a successful "Madam Curie." However, God called her into ordained ministry, and she became the first woman ordained by the Korean language Presbytery of the PCUSA in 1992.

In the third section of the book, Korean American Sermons, Rev. Irene Pak's "Standing Tall" is a theological reflection that weaves the story of the bent-over woman in the Gospel of Luke with Pak's own personal story. She shares how she learned to stand tall in the midst of sexism and racism through the healing touch of Christ.

Rev. Joann Haejong Lee reflects on Advent in "What to Expect When You're Expecting." Advent is Lee's favorite season in the church calendar, and she shared this sermon with her congregation when she was eight months pregnant with her first son. While Lee's pregnancy connected her to this "season of waiting" in a particularly profound way, she knew all people needed a sense of meaningful connection.

Rev. Yena K. Hwang offers us two sermons, "Discerning Kairos" and "words, words, words...and the Word." She prepared both sermons to be preached at the Presbytery of the National Capital during the year she served the presbytery as moderator. Hwang preached "Discerning Kairos" to close out her year as moderator, sharing the importance of discerning God's time as churches are challenged with many changes, and she encouraged presbyters to be filled with hope through those changes. The sermon "words, words, words... and the Word," is a poetic prose sermon, preached at the presbytery meeting where the ordination equality debate was on the docket. Hwang desired the sermon to encourage Spirit-filled discussions instead of mean-spirited debates on this important issue of justice and equality.

We hope the words in this book will inspire, challenge, and motivate you to make changes in your communities, churches, and homes. We hope, by the power of the Holy Spirit, these simple offerings will encourage people to stand up against injustices of racism and sexism that manifest themselves in overt and subtle ways. Racism and sexism are problems our churches need to address and we need to help dismantle. As we work toward a more just and equal society, we can be inspired by the courage shown by our foremothers who dared to make a new home in a foreign land, who dared to dream of a brighter future and strong faith in God for their daughters and sons. We can take delight in their stories and see our stories adding richness to theirs. We present these offerings of ourselves as a thanksgiving to all who have struggled before us so we can be here today. Praise be to God!

NOTES

1. Eleazar S. Fernandez, "American from the Hearts of a Diasporized People," in *Realizing the America of Our Hearts: Theological Voices of Asian Americans*, edited by Fumitaka Matsuoka & Eleazar S. Fernandez (St. Louis: Chalice Press, 2003), 256.

2. Sucheng Chan, *Asian Americans: An Interpretive History* (New York: Twayne Publishers, 1991), 15.

3. Gary Y. Okihiro, *Margins and Mainstreams: Asians in American History and Culture* (Seattle: University of Washington Press, 1994), 77.

History of Korean American Presbyterian Clergywomen (KAPCW)[1]

UNZU LEE

"KAPCW has always been a sanctuary to me—a place and time where I am able to give and receive support and love from other Korean American women pastors. . . . Being a member of KAPCW reminds me that I have a responsibility and a privilege to be an active part of a sisterhood that is uniquely called to serve Christ with passion, justice, and love." —REV. THERESA CHO, ST. JOHN'S PRESBYTERIAN CHURCH, SAN FRANCISCO, CALIFORNIA

"KAPCW means sisterhood. I am a member because I feel accepted, nurtured, mentored, and understood by my sisters who walk along with me in this journey called ministry." —REV. YENA HWANG, FORMER ASSOCIATE PASTOR, WHEATON COMMUNITY CHURCH, SILVER SPRING, MARYLAND

"Just the existence of KAPCW is a comfort and encouragement to me. We are sisters most deeply because of the grace of God and a shared calling to ministry. I value the friendships that I have made through the opportunities that KAPCW has provided." —REV. SUE KIM-AHN, MINISTER OF COMMUNITY LIFE, MENLO PARK PRESBYTERIAN CHURCH, MENLO PARK, CALIFORNIA

As of April 2012, more than ninety women of Korean ancestry have been ordained as teaching elders in the Presbyterian Church (USA). Additionally, there are about sixteen inquirers and eighteen candidates on the ordination track.[2] Organized in 1991, KAPCW is primarily a network of and for Korean American women in the Presbyterian Church who are ordained or seeking ordination as teaching elders in the PC(USA).

KAPCW's mission is to affirm, empower, and advocate for Korean American clergywomen in the PC(USA). KAPCW's purpose has been evolving. Its current purpose is as follows:

- To come together and celebrate our common ministry in Jesus Christ
- To support the network and to advocate for concerns of Korean American women in theology and ministry
- To enhance and educate for the leadership of Korean American clergywomen
- To connect members with each other between meetings
- To provide a place for sharing resources
- To network with related bodies in the PC(USA) and others on local, national, and global levels

What follows is KAPCW's history and what KAPCW has done in order to fulfill its purpose since its inception.

Beginnings

Seven Korean American women in ministry in the PC(USA) gathered in Louisville, Kentucky, on September 20–23, 1990, at the invitation of two General Assembly Council (GAC) ministry offices: the Korean Congregational Enhancement Office and the Office of Asian Leader Development. The initiative came about as a response to women's struggle for ordination that was being waged at the time by women in the Presbyterian Church of Korea (PCK)—a struggle that was started in 1933 by the Women's Missionary Society in the Presbytery of Ham-Nam.[3] The seven women were Rev. Jung Mi Han, Rev. Soon-Hwa Sun, Rev. Kaeja Cho, Rev. Shin-Hwa Park, Rev. Sang Wha Kim, Hang Ja Koo, and Soo Hoon Lee. Those who gathered shared a heartfelt concern about the emerging needs of the growing number of Korean American women in ministry and responded positively to the vision of becoming a nationally organized group.

This group of women called for the first national organizing meeting to be held in Los Angeles, California, on May 23–25, 1991, under the theme "The Prophetic Role of Korean American Clergywomen in the Twenty-first Century." Eight additional women responded to this call. Among the fifteen women gathered, the new clergywomen were Rev. Mary Paik, Rev. Jean Kim, Rev. Elizabeth Kwon, and Rev. Susan Hong, and the candidates were Marion Park, Unzu Lee, Myung Ja Yue, and Mickie Choi. This organizing conference was supported by a number of GAC agencies, and Mary Ann Lundy, then director of the Women's Ministry Unit, presented the keynote address. Other staff and elected people who provided leadership at this event included Rev. Sun Bai Kim (GAC), Rev. Paul Chun (National Korean Presbyterian Council [NKPC]), now National Council of Korean Presbyterian Churches [NCKPC], Rev. Soo Kyung Cho, Rev. Chang Wook Choi (GAC), and Elder Yong Il Cho (NKPC).

Gathered for the first time as an ethnic group of Korean American women in ministry in the Presbyterian Church (USA), we were a very diverse group in terms of age, language skills, ministry context, and theological perspectives. While realizing that many differences might divide us, we affirmed that we were sisters in Christ who had received the call to be his witnesses and decided to become one another's companions on our journey of faith and ministry. Korean American Clergywomen PC(USA) was officially organized on May 24, 1991, and five women, who included three regional representatives, a secretary, and a treasurer, were elected to provide leadership for the organization. Over time, it became known as Korean American Presbyterian Clergywomen (KAPCW), and we did away with geographic representation and the position of secretary. The three women in three classes who formed the coordinating team assumed the leadership responsibilities, with the exception of finances. This leadership structure stayed intact until 2010, when the KAPCW board was formed.

Annual Conferences

KAPCW has held an annual conference since it was organized in 1991, and the conference has been open to any woman of Korean heritage in the Presbyterian Church (USA) (and partner churches) engaged in ministry or considering ministry as a vocation. These annual conferences have served multiple purposes for Korean American women in ministry, and in the following we offer a brief description of each conference.

LOS ANGELES, CALIFORNIA, MAY 21–23, 1992

We returned to Los Angeles for another gathering and were confronted with the reality of the aftermath of *sa-i-gu*.[4] The conference was organized in a storytelling format. We told stories by responding to the questions "Where was I?" "Where am I?" and "Where will I be?" In hearing out each other's stories, we shed many tears and connected to one another heart to heart.

THE MERCY CENTER, BURLINGAME, CALIFORNIA, APRIL 13–15, 1993

Realizing that the baggage we carry often has undue influence on our ministry, we gathered under the theme "Flying with Baggage." Dr. Jung Ha Kim, professor at Georgia State University with a degree in the sociology of religion, helped us unpack some of the baggage that we carry as Korean American women, and together we sought ways to become liberated from the baggage.

PAJARO DUNES, CALIFORNIA, APRIL 6–9, 1994

For almost two millennia since Jesus, the church has not allowed women to become spiritual leaders, because the church has historically identified women with nature/body rather than with spirit/logos. Our biology became our destiny. For this reason, we chose "Women's Body and Spirituality" as our theme for this conference. We reflected on this theme from biblical, biochemical, and conceptual perspectives. Jeannette Wei, who studied acupressure in China and has done a lot of work around healing using both the Eastern wisdom and Christian teachings on the body, served as our resource person. The waters of the Pacific Ocean, which touches Korea, our motherland, refreshed our bodies.

REV. SANG WHA KIM'S HOME, PALMDALE, CALIFORNIA, APRIL 24–27, 1995

Realizing that Rev. Sang Wha Kim had missed the conference in 1993 due to her serious health concerns, we decided to go to her house for our conference. In addition to worship, prayer, and community building, we shared with one another the current issues we face as clergywomen, reflected on the challenges we face as Asian American women, made masks to get in touch with our self-image, and had a session on time management. At this gathering we decided that in the future we would intentionally meet on seminary campuses in order to connect with the Korean American women students there and to be a resource for them.

SAN FRANCISCO THEOLOGICAL SEMINARY, SAN ANSELMO, CALIFORNIA, APRIL 29–MAY 2, 1996

Dr. Elizabeth Liebert, Director of Spiritual Formation at San Francisco Theological Seminary, provided leadership. In addition to sharing time in worship, Bible study, and community building, we had a session on "Women and the Ordination Process" led by Rev. Mary Paik, and we also viewed slides taken by Rev. Unzu Lee at the Fourth United Nations

Conference on Women in Beijing, China, in September 1995. We visited the Cameron House in Chinatown, San Francisco, a multiservice agency serving Asian communities in the Bay Area since it was started in 1874 by Donaldina Cameron, a Presbyterian woman abolitionist. We designated May 1 as Students' Day.

PRINCETON THEOLOGICAL SEMINARY, PRINCETON, NEW JERSEY, MARCH 10–13, 1997

Su Yon Pak, an EdD student at Union Seminary's joint program with Columbia University in New York, led sessions on singing as a spiritual practice. Elder Evelyn Hwang, Associate for Preparation for Ministry, led a session on the ordination process. During the business meeting we nominated Rev. Jean Kim for the "Women of Faith" award. (She was selected and received the award at the Women of Faith Breakfast held during the 1997 General Assembly.)

MCCORMICK THEOLOGICAL SEMINARY, CHICAGO, ILLINOIS, MARCH 23–26, 1998

Our sister Rev. Mary Paik arranged for us to meet at McCormick. The focus theme was "Liturgy and Spirituality." Rev. Linda Wygant led several sessions on the theme. Elder Evelyn Hwang led a session on preparation for and the process of ordination in the PC(USA). On the evening of March 24 a panel and dialogue were held with Korean male students at McCormick facilitated by Professor Hearn Chun. Additionally, we heard from the executive director of Korean American Women in Need (KAN-WIN) about the situation of domestic violence in Korean immigrant communities and made visits to agencies serving homeless people.

CARLSBAD SEAPOINTE RESORT, CARLSBAD, CALIFORNIA, MARCH 24–27, 1999

Meeting by the sea, we enjoyed God's goodness in nature, one another's company, and a lot of wonderful seafood.

(While there is no Presbyterian seminary in southern Calfornia, we chose that location because it was home to Korean American clergywomen who were doing ministry.) The focus of this conference was visioning. Rev. Carol Shellenburger led the visioning process for us over three sessions. There was much discussion on how we need to become more intentional about identifying common issues we face and sharing helpful resources we may have come across or developed ourselves. We raised as a concern the absence of the first-generation Korean American clergywomen in our gathered community. We generated ideas that might help us become a more cohesive and supportive group that celebrates our common ministry. We very much appreciated the generosity of Rev. Dr. Mickie Choi, who opened up her condominium for our stay during the conference.

NOVATO, CALIFORNIA, MARCH 29–APRIL 1, 2000

"Let Us Celebrate" was the theme of our tenth anniversary conference. Rev. Ann Rhee-Menzie offered her wonderful house for our use, and we had a record attendance of more than thirty participants. In addition to laughing, praying, worshiping, and studying the Bible together, we created long lists of project ideas and tasks to strengthen the organization. We held the tenth anniversary community worship celebration at the Korean Presbyterian Church of San Rafael. Our site visit was to the San Francisco Network Ministries in the Tenderloin District in San Francisco. We also had a time in which to share the resources that we had brought with us.

DUMAS BAY CENTER, SEATTLE, WASHINGTON, MARCH 21–24, 2001

We met in the hometown of Rev. Jean Kim. This conference was framed as a spiritual retreat, and Rev. Marjorie Hoyer-Smith, who was on the faculty in the spiritual direction program at San Francisco Theological Seminary, provided leadership. We participated in various spiritual practices using our body, mind, and soul. The Church of Mary Magdalene, the church started by Rev. Jean Kim for homeless women, was the choice for our site visit.

UNION PRESBYTERIAN SEMINARY, RICHMOND, VIRGINIA, FEBRUARY 27–MARCH 2, 2002

Rev. Dr. Syngman Rhee and Heasun Rhee served as generous hosts to us for this conference. Realizing that part of our struggle has to do with not having written texts to validate our truths as women because the privilege of theological writing has belonged principally to men over the last two thousand years, we came to Union Seminary to learn to tell our story through writing. Under the guidance of Rev. Dr. Katie Cannon, professor of ethics at Union Presbyterian Seminary, we learned the "hows" of writing autobiographical theology, and then we wrote our own autobiographical theologies and shared them with one another. In appreciation for Dr. Cannon's leadership, we sent a $500 gift to Daughters of Zelophehad ministry.

UNION THEOLOGICAL SEMINARY, NEW YORK, NEW YORK, MARCH 19–22, 2003

We gathered in a worship space set by Rev. Mary Paik with a long, wavy blue cloth on the floor and votive candles along its edges. Using the biblical story of the Hebrews' conquest of and settlement in the promised land of Canaan, we reflected on the journeys of settlement that we have been on since we left our homeland. "Whiteness" was a conceptual framework used for this reflection, and we used Eric Law's photo language to help us explore the theme. One bonus of meeting in New York City was the chance to visit the United Nations. We were treated to a wonderful dinner by the dean of Auburn Seminary, Rev. Dr. Lee Hancock, and we engaged in dialogue with her about how KAPCW could serve as a resource to Auburn's educational endeavors. Rev. Mary McNamara, who is the vice president of Union Theological Seminary also invited us into her home for tea. All of this was made possible because of our Korean American sister Dr. Su Yon Pak, who was on staff at Union Seminary.

EPISCOPAL DIVINITY SCHOOL, CAMBRIDGE, MASSACHUSETTS, MARCH 17–20, 2004

Rev. Joan Martin, a teaching elder in the PC(USA) and professor of ethics at Episcopal Divinity School, was our contact resource person, and we met in one of the school's buildings that is used for functions such as retreats. We reflected on *A Step from Heaven* by An Na, a Korean American author, and participated in a *lectio divina* art project led by Theresa Cho. Through the process, each of us created a journal book, wrote our own stories, and shared our stories with one another. Members of the Korean Church of Boston and its pastor, Rev. Young Ghil Lee, treated us to many wonderful meals. We felt affirmed and appreciated! We left Boston with grateful hearts.

MCCORMICK THEOLOGICAL SEMINARY, CHICAGO, ILLINOIS, APRIL 13–16, 2005

Rev. Mary Paik, serving as vice president for student affairs, arranged for us to meet at McCormick. Given that the Presbyterian Church was celebrating the ordination of women as deacons, elders, and ministers, we met under the theme "Our Ethnic Identity and Ministry." Rev. Unzu Lee served as "provocateur" for our dialogue and reflection on the issues of ordination, ethnicity, and communities of accountability. We visited homeless shelters, and Rev. Kim, the godmother of homeless ministry in the PC(USA), educated us on ministering to and with homeless women.

MCCORMICK THEOLOGICAL SEMINARY, CHICAGO, ILLINOIS, MAY 9–12, 2006

KAPCW's request that McCormick provide us with free lodging and facility use for our annual conferences for the next three years (2006–2008) was positively received. So, we met at McCormick again. Professor Jae Won Lee led several Bible study sessions for us, and we went to Night Ministry, a nondenominational agency that serves the most vulnerable in Chicago, for our site visit. Rev. Ann Rhee-Menzie brought to our attention the recent incidents of domestic violence involving homicide in the Korean immigrant communities. She told us that she as a minister has come to realize that she cannot do this work alone, and that churches need to teach and preach against domestic violence. In response, during its business meeting KAPCW made a decision to become a partner with the *Shimtuh* of the Korean Community Center of East Bay and participate in its "Healthy Family" campaign by developing a Bible study curriculum addressing the issue. Several members of KAPCW volunteered to participate as writers, and KAPCW made a commitment to cover the cost of one meeting of the writing team.

MCCORMICK THEOLOGICAL SEMINARY, CHICAGO, ILLINOIS, MAY 16–19, 2007

Meeting under the theme "Wounded Healers," we reviewed a draft copy of the Bible study written by some of our members and shared our feedback. Some of the first-comers to the conference were currently doing doctoral work in Christian education, and they contributed much with their critiques and recommendations as educators. For our site visit, we visited Night Ministry for the second year in a row. McCormick extended our contract for three more years through 2010.

MCCORMICK THEOLOGICAL SEMINARY, CHICAGO, ILLINOIS, MAY 21–24, 2008

Meeting under the theme "Hand in Hand: Redefining Ministry Together," we engaged in the practice of hands meditation, created an image that symbolizes ministry using Play-Doh, and participated in a panel discussion on "Various Hands of Ministry"; we concluded the process by redefining ministry through biblical and theological reflection. Our site visit was to the Interfaith Worker Justice, a nonprofit agency that since 1996 has been organizing, educating, and advocating on issues at the intersection of faith and labor.

MCCORMICK THEOLOGICAL SEMINARY, CHICAGO, ILLINOIS, MAY 26–29, 2009

We gathered to share our stories, laughter, and ministry experiences under the theme "Preach It, Sister!" Rev. Alma Crawford, a United Church of Christ clergywoman who has taught preaching in one of the schools of the Graduate Theological Union, served as our guest resource person and preacher. Our own Rev. Joann Lee and Rev. Yena K. Hwang delivered inspiring sermons during worship, and we were richly blessed. We also practiced exegetical skills and shared with one another our sermon preparation process and tools. Jieun Kim Han, who is theologically trained and who was working as Church Leadership Connection Consultant in Louisville at the time, walked us through the process of writing, preparing, and filing our Personal Information Forms, and the matching process available through the church. At this conference we decided to create a board for KAPCW. We chose three women to do the preparatory work for creating a board.

MCCORMICK THEOLOGICAL SEMINARY, CHICAGO, ILLINOIS, MAY 25–27, 2010

Those nominated to the board met on May 24–25 to create a leadership structure for the board and develop bylaws. Rev. Yena K. Hwang was chosen as president of the KAPCW board. The conference started on May 25 under the theme "Through the Looking Glass." Participants were asked to spend intentional time in self-reflection and contemplation, to reconnect with God residing within themselves, and to reflect on the many roles and identities that we hold as we seek out God's image in the plurality of our relationships. The *kim-bap* that we made together for our picnic lunch by Lake Michigan was the best!

MEADOWKIRK RETREAT CENTER, MIDDLEBURG, VIRGINIA, MAY 24–27, 2011

We held a board meeting on May 23–24 immediately prior to the conference. Marking the twentieth anniversary of KAPCW, we gathered under the theme "20 Years of KAPCW: Call of the WILD (Women in Leadership and Development)." We had a wonderful time together at this beautiful, verdant setting, with moving worship, good food, laughter, thoughtful and engaging theological reflections, and many opportunities to enjoy God's goodness. A Bible study session titled "A Time for Looking Back," led by Rev. Margee Iddings, a professional spiritual director, was an especially wonderful and affecting experience.

The highlight of this retreat was the twentieth anniversary community worship attended not only by us, but also by many members of the Wheaton Community Church and some minister members of the National Capital Presbytery. Among them was Elder Cindy Bolbach, moderator of the 219th General Assembly. Elder Bolbach preached, and women of Wheaton Church blessed us with their singing. Many people and entities blessed us with many gifts. The National Capital Presbytery and the Rev. Sun Bai Kim sent us a congratulatory letter on the occasion of KAPCW's twentieth anniversary.

SAN FRANCISCO THEOLOGICAL SEMINARY, SAN FRANCISCO, CALIFORNIA, MAY 22–25, 2012

We held a board meeting the day before the conference began. The theme of the conference, "Generations: Wisdom for the Ages," was focused around the different generations and how we value those past, present, and future in our midst following God's call in their lives. We watched *The Joy Luck Club* together and reflected together the different emotions that arose in us from the movie. Rev. Diana Cheifetz also came and led us in a time of spiritual direction all together. Because we were in the Bay Area, we also took a ferry to Angel Island

and learned the history of that island, where many Asian immigrants came to the United States. We toured the pier of San Francisco, and we enjoyed a nice meal of crab and seafood together. We played games, shared stories, and affirmed one another through words that were then melted onto candles. Each woman took home a candle with her name on it and affirmations written by her sisters in faith.

CARNIVAL CRUISE, DEPARTING CALIFORNIA, APRIL 15–19, 2013

We held our annual conference on a cruise ship under the theme "Claiming the *Ajumma* Within." Our sister Nayoung Ha, a PhD candidate at the Lutheran School of Theology at Chicago, proposed "*Ajumma* Theology" as an empowering framework for speaking truth to power and engaging in justice. During the conference, we discovered the *Ajumma* within each of us and connected her with biblical *Ajummas*. We held discussion groups, shared fellowship, networked, and did some sightseeing. It was a great experience to relax on a cruise ship and also gain some theological insight on what it means to be Asian American women in ministry.

UNION PRESBYTERIAN SEMINARY, RICHMOND, VIRGINIA, JUNE 3–6, 2014

With the theme "To Journey Within," we gathered at Union Presbyterian Seminary, hosted by Rev. Dr. Sung Hee Chang, director of Asian American Ministry Center and assistant professor of Christian education at the seminary. Our guest speaker and retreat leader was Dr. Maria Clark Fleshood, an Imago Relationship Therapist, who led us in an in-depth exploration of what wrappings we have placed around ourselves and how they have hindered us from the more complete discovery and celebration of being made whole in God's image. We engaged in mindful meditation, learned how our "imago" is developed and how brain development influences imago-image, and we explored ways to become more conscious, critically engaging negative and unhealthy belief systems and behaviors to help us reach our great potential to live out our calling to its fullest potential.

Support, Networking, Education, and Advocacy

SUPPORT FOR AND NETWORKING AMONG KOREAN AMERICAN WOMEN IN MINISTRY

We have intentionally met on seminary campuses for a number of years in order to connect with Korean American women students in theological schools and to be a resource for them. We have provided educational sessions on the ordination process and the call process led by General Assembly staff. Senior members try to serve as mentors to emerging ministers. KAPCW has always offered scholarships to those interested in attending its annual conference. We also provide for childcare in order to facilitate the participation of women with children.

The Rev. Eun Joo Kim sends out a monthly e-mail to all the women who are included in her e-list. The monthly note highlights personal milestones, news about network members, call for prayers, information about events and employment opportunities, and more. We have also used social media, such as Facebook, to promote connection.

KAPCW gifted each new ordinand with a clergy gown in 1991–1995. Since 1995, KAPCW has sent a *saek-dong* stole to each new ordinand if she has attended the KAPCW conference at least once. Women survivors of domestic violence make the stoles. Thanks to grants made by KAPCW, three seminary students attended the Racial Ethnic Convocation in Albuquerque, New Mexico, in 1996.

Since KAPCW's beginning, we have tried in various ways to identify and connect with Korean American women in ministry in the Presbyterian Church (USA). In June 1993 a request was sent to all the presbyteries in the church that they provide us with the names and addresses of all women of Korean ancestry who are clergy, inquirers, and candidates. For the last five or six years we have maintained a practice of sending a communication to every Korean congregation, to presbyteries, and to theological schools asking them to share our annual conference information with Korean American women who are ordained, in the ordination process, or matriculating in theological studies.

NETWORKING AND PARTNERSHIP WITH OTHER ENTITIES

At each conference we share reports from the National Korean Presbyterian Women (NKPW), National Council of Korean Presbyterian Churches (NCKPC), National Asian Presbyterian Women (NAPW), and other entities. We discuss our relationships with those organizations and determine ways to network and be in partnership with them. Over the years KAPCW has related to NCKPC by sending its annual conference report either through a member attending the NKPC annual conference or by mail.

On October 21, 1995, KAPCW sent a congratulatory letter and a Communion set to the president of the Women Ministers Association of the Presbyterian Church of Korea (KPC) on the occasion of the approval of women's ordination amendment which ended the struggle begun in 1933.

Korean American clergywomen attending the Presbyterian Women's triennial gathering in 2003 held an official breakfast meeting with the fifteen clergywomen of the Presbyterian Church in Korea who participated in the gathering.

In 2007–2009 Rev. Jean Kim, Rev. Eun Joo Kim, and Rev. Unzu Lee served on a special committee created by NKPC to study the status of women's leadership in Korean American churches. The three served as major contributors to the report. The report and recommendations were adopted by NCKPC in 2009 at its annual meeting in Baltimore, Maryland, and have been published both in Korean and English. Rev. Unzu Lee and Rev. Jean Kim served as their editors.

Rev. Jean Kim has served as chairperson of the Women's Advocacy Committee, a standing committee of NCKPC created in 2009 when the aforementioned report was received by NCKPC.

KAPCW contributes to laywomen's empowerment by appointing one of its members to serve as a spiritual advisor to NKPW. Rev. Unzu Lee, Rev. Ann Menzie, and Rev. Heeja Han have served in the past. Rev. Jung Sook Kim is currently serving in this role, and Rev. Unzu Lee is serving as the chair of NKPW's Education Committee.[5]

KAPCW members are increasingly providing leadership for NKPW as well as presbytery and synod Korean Presbyterian Women (KPW) groups. In the fall of 2011 Rev. Jihyun Oh served as the coordinator for the women's leadership education program offered through Columbia Theological Seminary under the sponsorship of NKPW. Heidi Park, a PhD student at Claremont and a candidate for ordination in the PC(USA), Rev. Unzu Lee, and Rev. Jihyun Oh served as faculty. Three other faculty members were Rev. David Hoonjin Chai, Rev. Paul Huh, and Rev. Seung Hae Yoo (United Methodist Church).

ADVOCACY

Upon hearing the news not only that the overture for women's ordination was again defeated at the 76th General Assembly of the Korean Presbyterian Church, but also that a moratorium on this issue was imposed for three years, our leadership team made a decision to send the Korean Presbyterian Church a statement expressing our disappointment and calling the church to faithfully reconsider its decision.

In response to the brutal sexual assault and murder of Ms. Yoon Kum-I by U.S. Army Pvt. Kenneth Markle, KAPCW took the following actions: (1) the Coordinating Team of KAPCW communicated its concern to the GAC staff in Louisville; (2) it sent a letter to President Bill Clinton raising concerns about violence perpetrated against Korean women by the U.S. military personnel stationed in South Korea; (3) KAPCW sent a donation of $100.00 to the Joint Commission for Counter Measures regarding Yoon Kum-I's murder case in Korea.

PROJECTS

As mentioned earlier, in 2006 KAPCW made a decision to become a partner of *Shimtuh* in its "Healthy Family" campaign. The project that we chose was to develop a Bible study curriculum. The writers of the Bible study *Healthy Christian Family* were Nayoung Ha, a PhD student at Lutheran Seminary and candidate for ordination in the PC(USA), Rev. Yena Hwang, Hye Young Lee (social worker with an MDiv from McCormick), and Rev. Unzu Lee. The draft was completed in 2007, but it sat on the shelf due to lack of funding. In 2009 *Shimtuh* received a grant from the Robert Wood Johnson Foundation, and that breathed new energy into the project. Under the leadership of Rev. Ann Rhee Menzie, a staff member of *Shimtuh*, two teams (one team to review the content and one team to edit) consisting of local ministers, educators, and practitioners in the area of domestic violence were created. They were Rev. Kyung Soo Kim, Rev. Chul Woo Kwon, Rev. Moon Chul Kim, Joy Church, James Choi, Sophia Kim, Rev. Julie Kim, and Rev. Moon Young Choi. The outline of the Bible study is as follows:

- In the Image of God (Genesis 1:26-31; 2:18-25)
- Mutual Respect (Ephesians 5:21-33)
- Mutual Accountability (Deuteronomy 24:1-4; Mathew 19:1-12)
- The Power of Love (Luke 10:25-37)
- Suffering Neighbor (John 9:1-12)
- Forgiveness and Accountability (Matthew 18:15-35)
- Toward Wholeness (Luke 8:43-48)
- Instrument of Healing (Mark 2:1-12)
- Proclaiming God's Realm (Isaiah 61:1-3a)

This edited version was pilot tested in five church groups. To put the curriculum to a final test, three groups of people with different demographic characteristics—a young adult group, a single mom's group, a mixed group—have tried out the curriculum, and one more group will study it before it is ready for publication. This curriculum is now available in both Korean and English.

As We Move Forward

The twenty-five years of our journey would not have been possible without God's faithful guiding hand. To the God of Miriam and Moses we offer our praise of thanksgiving.

Other individuals and entities have accompanied us along the way with their support. Among them are women's groups in Korean immigrant churches, institutional agencies, theological schools, synods, presbyteries, and individuals. The Korean church women's groups that have supported us include National Korean Presbyterian Women (NKPW), Korean Presbyterian Women (KPW) in the Synod of the Covenant, KPW of the Korean Presbyterian Church of Metro Detroit, KPW of Wheaton Community Church, and KPW of the Korean Church of Boston, to name a few. The PC(USA) agencies and offices that have supported us include the Korean Congregational Support office, the Women's Ministries Program Area, and the Presbyterians for Investment and Loan program. The Synod of the Covenant has gifted us with a grant every year over a number of years, and the Presbytery of San Jose and many theological schools have supported us along the way with many in-kind gifts. We offer them our gratitude.

KAPCW functioned as a membership organization in its first twenty years. This means that everyone who attended the annual conference and who paid her membership dues was given full voice and a vote at the annual business meeting that took place during its annual conference. In 2010, however, KAPCW created a board, and all decision-making power is now vested in the board. The following members were elected to the board of directors: Rev. Heeja Han, Rev. Yena Hwang (president), Rev. Eun Joo Kim (vice-president), Rev. Dr. Grace Ji-Sun Kim, Rev. Jean Kim, Rev. Jung Sook Kim (treasurer), Rev. Joann Lee, Rev. Ann Rhee Menzie (secretary), Rev. Unzu Lee (historian), Rev. Irene Pak, Rev. Mary Paik (development officer), Rev. Marion Park, and Rev. Kyung Moon Yoon. With the creation of the board, KAPCW has begun a new chapter of its journey. As KAPCW's leadership team, the board wishes to develop KAPCW into a network/organization that might serve as a home and source of encouragement to Korean American women in ministry, who often feel alone and isolated.

As already mentioned, the number of Korean American women ordained in the church as teaching elders has increased from a mere handful in 1991 to more than ninety,[6] and this trend is bound to continue because as many as sixteen inquirers and eighteen candidates are currently pursuing ordination. Among these, eleven have a doctoral degree (PhD, MD, and EdD), and nine are PhD students.

Out of the ninety-three clergywomen who have been accounted for by KAPCW, four of them—Rev. Elizabeth Kwon, Rev. Soon Hwa Sun, Rev. Soon Bok Lee, and Rev. Sang Wha Kim—have already completed their earthly journeys and joined the cloud of witnesses over the horizon. Seven women have honorably retired, and about ten women are not actively engaged in ministry right now. Those of us who are currently engaged are serving in the following contexts: 34 as teaching elders in parishes (15 in Korean immigrant churches, 17 white or multiethnic churches, and 2 in Korea); 14 as chaplains in hospitals, hospices, university, and the military; 7 as faculty in theological schools (2 in Korea); 5 in specialized ministries through nonprofit agencies; 3 as missionaries; and 3 as executives in PC(USA) agencies. Among those who are working in parishes, only one is a head of staff, and a number of them are working part-time as temporary supply.

The foregoing description reveals a few unique traits of the Korean American women in ministry:

- Korean American clergywomen are a heterogeneous group. Those who work in the parish make up less than a half of the total number. A great number of Korean American women in ministry are engaged in so-called specialized ministries.
- Among those who are in the parish, more women are serving predominantly white or multiethnic congregations than Korean immigrant churches.
- The number of Korean American clergywomen who are serving in Korean immigrant churches make up less than 20 percent of the total number, and among them, one-third are involved in either children's or English ministry.
- Korean American women in ministry are highly educated.[7]
- A significant number of Korean American women in ministry are in the childbearing and childrearing stage of their lives. Unlike most men in ministry, a great number of Korean American women in ministry choose to take a leave from ministry to care for their child/children. This leave ranges from a few months to ten years or more.

These traits, even in a limited way, inform us about the situation of Korean American women in ministry. Though many of us are products of the Korean immigrant churches, many of us are not serving Korean Presbyterians. One clergywoman who is currently serving a predominantly white congregation yearns, "I really want to retire having served at least one Korean congregation as a solo or senior pastor." At age fifty, she has been in ministry for more than two decades. Will she be granted that opportunity during her lifetime?

As NCKPC celebrates its fortieth anniversary, the writer of this report cannot help but remember the journey taken by the Hebrews from Egypt to Canaan. Like Joshua, who represented the emerging generation of the Hebrews who grew up during their sojourn in the wilderness, many of us belong to the emerging generations of Korean immigrants who have grown up in the Korean immigrant churches during the last forty years. On the one hand, we are actively engaged in various types of ministry, and many of us are playing many significant roles in the larger church. On the other hand, to a great extent we remain invisible in the Korean immigrant church context. Many of us are separated from the Korean immigrant context by the generational and gender gap, and we wonder what role we might be able to play in the next forty years.

We are thankful for the invitation to tell our stories at this important juncture of the history of NCKPC. As Korean American women in ministry in the Presbyterian Church (USA), we care very much about the future of Korean American Presbyterian churches. We pray that our story will inform all of us as we seek God's wisdom and guidance for the direction of our journey for the next forty years and more.

NOTES

1. A shorter version of this chapter appears in Paul Chun, ed., *A History of Korean American Church* [sic] *in the Presbyterian Church (U.S.A.): Celebrating the 40th Anniversary of the National Council of Korean Presbyterian Churches* (Seoul: National Council of Korean Presbyterian Churches, 2014), 236–56.

2. These numbers are approximations. The database of inquirers and candidates kept in the Office of the General Assembly (OGA) is completely dependent on the information submitted to the office by presbyteries, and presbyteries do not always correctly identify their inquirers and candidates by ethnicity. Moreover, ethnic identification is becoming increasingly difficult because of interracial marriages being on an upward trend. The OGA database for clergy uses racial, not ethnic, categories, and therefore there is no way of getting an accurate count of women of Korean ancestry ordained in the PC(USA). The data provided in this report comes from a compilation that KAPCW maintains.

3. The Presbyterian Church of Korea (PCK) divided into two in the early 1950's. The Presbyterian Church in the Republic of Korea (PROK) which was organized in 1954 started ordaining women as elders in 1956 and as ministers in 1974.

4. *Sa-i-gu*, which means "four-two-nine," is what Koreans call the civil unrest that was set off on April 29, 1992, when a mostly white jury found four Los Angeles Police Department officers not guilty of assault with a deadly weapon and excessive force against twenty-five-year-old Rodney King following a high-speed chase

on March 3, 1991. The city's Korean immigrant community sustained nearly half of the $1 billion in property damage caused by the riots; the dreams and pride of more than ten thousand Korean shopkeepers and their families were reduced to ash in the conflagration, including 2,300 predominantly Korean-owned businesses in South Los Angeles alone. Many of those businesses never returned, casualties of the riots' political aftermath.

5. Rev. Jung Sook Kim and Rev. Unzu Lee have completed their terms. Rev. Soon Hee Earm and Rev. Kyung Moon Yoon are now serving respectively as Spiritual Advisor and as chairperson of the Education Committee of NKPW.

6. One of them is a commissioned lay pastor.

7. A number of Korean American women who are currently pursuing a PhD in theological schools or universities are either ordained or are candidates for ordination.

PART I

Theological Reflections

1

The Passage toward Parenthood as Vocational Practice

MIHEE KIM-KORT

"To look deep into your child's eyes and see in him both yourself and something utterly strange, and then to develop a zealous attachment to every aspect of him, is to achieve parenthood's self-regarding, yet unselfish, abandon. It is astonishing how often such mutuality had been realized—how frequently parents who had supposed that they couldn't care for an exceptional child discover that they can. The parental predisposition to love prevails in the most harrowing of circumstances. There is more imagination in the world than one might think." —ANDREW SOLOMON[1]

Working through Solomon's critically acclaimed book, *Far from the Tree: Parents, Children, and the Search for Identity*, I am struck with how much it allows my own story to emerge in memories that had disappeared from the surface of my heart. I remember being in high school and my mother and I fighting about some minutia. She would interrupt me in one of my tirades with, "I can't wait for YOU to have a daughter someday!"—as if I would never truly understand her side of the story until I became a mother.

She was right.

My little girl, Anna, at the time of this writing is a little over three years old, and I already feel the blessing and curse that my own mother uttered to me about having a daughter, and about having children in general. But something unique is happening between Anna and me. I see so much of her unique personality, but I also see so much of myself in her, and this both frightens and thrills me. It makes me understand why my mother had that secret, self-satisfied smile on her face every time I would ask the question "Why?" She would reply, "You'll see. Oh, just wait. You'll see how hard it is to have a daughter."

> In the heat of an argument, my mother once told me, "Someday you can go to a therapist and tell him all about how your terrible mother ruined your life. But it will be your ruined life you're talking about. So make a life for yourself in which you can feel happy, and in which you can love and be loved, because that's what's actually important." You can love someone but not accept him; you can accept someone but not love him. I wrongly felt the flaws in my parents' acceptance as deficits in their love. Now, I think their primary experience was of having a child who spoke a language they'd never thought of studying.[2]

I had forgotten this exchange as my husband and I began to move toward having a family. We tried to conceive, and it didn't seem to go our way. We then tried fertility medication. All the while, friends around us seemed to be getting pregnant so easily. It was a difficult time to live, all the more so whenever someone tried to encourage and appease me by saying, "You're a mother already to the children and youth in your ministry," when all I could think about was how much I wanted a daughter or a son of my own. All I could think about was how desperately I wanted to be a mother.

And then I finally conceived, and we had twins. Soon after we had a huge surprise: child number three. We became parents of three children in the span of three years, and our world turned upside down. I became a mostly stay-at-home mother, and it was vastly different from what I envisioned my life would be as a minister and as a parent. Yet, even through the fog and haze of new babies, lost sleep, and the physical grind of raising children, I found that this time was rich with meaning and significance for me, particularly as a woman who seeks to work for social justice and to bring God's kingdom to bear in this broken and hungry world. Specifically, at every turn I slowly began to see the ways this time and experience would contribute to my shaping and development as a pastor and as a person of faith. In fact, this began even before we had the children.

Vocational Discernment: Being Faithful in the Struggle

I'm trying not to look at the timer on my watch, and so I'm running around doing anything to avoid the bathroom for three minutes. I fold towels, and then I refold them. I make the bed we never make. I organize piles of paper into new piles, and then I move them around. I'm wiping down the desk and bookshelves with the sleeve of my sweatshirt and collecting as much dust as possible, as if it's the shimmery remains of fairies' wings. The more fairy dust, the better the chances for those barely whispered wishes and sighs that have left my lips.

Finally, I let myself look down at my watch. It's 3:09. I put the stick down at 3:06:47. With a few more grains of seconds left, I slowly walk back to the bathroom in measured steps, methodically counting them. I look at the sink where the pregnancy test is lying face up. I reach for it, breathing quickly, my stomach filling with fireworks and shooting stars that I try to squelch because it's always too early to celebrate anything.

I see: One. Blue. Line. Immediately, I toss the pregnancy test into the trashcan.

I lie down on the floor on my stomach, head in my arms, and close my eyes. I'm breathing in the chemicals of the floor and bathroom tile cleaner without a care because I have nothing in me to protect or to shield from outside toxins. I have no new life being formed in me to worry over. I begin to cry. Gasping for air, I turn over. It's only been a year. Some people try for ten years. I tell myself, "Get it together, girl. It could be worse. Way worse. We've only tried for twelve months. We've only just started the medication. We've only just started tracking the weeks."

"We've only . . ." These words, which have become a mantra of sorts, are not helping. I've memorized these words, and I say them perfectly each time, like the proper and necessary closure or a magic spell. It's an incantation that enables me eventually to rise from the bathroom floor like Lazarus from his tomb. Except the mantra isn't working now. Month after month for twelve months it's been a turbulent flight amidst skies that hold these hopes—nauseating and thrilling, exciting and disappointing. But, honestly, it's mostly soul-crushing. "It's only been . . ." doesn't make watching baptisms easier. "It's only been . . ." doesn't dilute the headache of Mother's Day. "It's only been . . ." doesn't keep my heart from shattering when I receive a surprise hug from a child or smell the top of a baby's head. "It's only been . . ." doesn't inure me to the stabs of agony any time I see a swollen belly or an infant seat.

But, I stand back up. "Only" finally works. Even if it's only one blue line, I have to get up. So, I find the calendar hanging on the wall and mark another day in the month ahead. We hold our breath in the weeks between as we count down the days. We make up stories about the strange cravings and miraculous expansion I will someday experience for those nine months. We dream, night and day, murmuring prayers for those two blue lines. . . .

I sit for the first time in a room that will eventually become like a second home. At the moment, though, I am struck by the nameless neutral color of the walls, and the contrast between the innocuous and clichéd prints of babies and puppies and the various posters of the female anatomy. I look around, and my eyes linger on the intimidating diagnostic machines, the lone chair for the assumed support person, and the red hazardous materials container, which together seem like an odd combination for decor. Andy stands next to me, somehow managing to look casual and jittery, which is accentuated by his 6'3" frame. I can almost feel him vibrating between the two emotions of casual and jittery next to me. I lie back and look up at the ceiling, where there is a poster of a bright blue ocean reminiscent of the beaches in the Dominican Republic. It seems bizarre at first, but its sedating effect on me slowly makes sense.

I suddenly feel very serious. It's a moment we've anticipated for almost two years now. *How much of this is wishful thinking? Have I made this all up? Are we really here?* My hands are tight with uncertainty, and I can feel my toes curling down as I try to hold in any feeling of anxiety and stress. The doctor walks in and, before she sits down, immediately starts chatting, "How are you feeling this morning?"

"Okay." I lick my lips, wishing I had my ChapStick. "A little anxious, I think," I mouth, dryly.

"Well, go ahead and lie back, and we'll take a look in there," she says as she puts on some rubber gloves and brings one machine with a screen much closer. "Your beta levels were perfect, so let's see what we have here."

The assistant, who I had forgotten was there, has turned off the lights. A foreign, yet soothing, humming noise comes on as the screen lights up. It was black, but there were white scribbles and a vague outline of a circle on the screen. And then, a sound—a steady throbbing.

"Okay," she says, "let's see." Her eyes are focused on the images, and she has a smile pulling at the corners of her mouth. "So, there's the embryo, and you can hear its heartbeat."

"Really?" I ask, straining to make sense of the little marble in the middle of the screen—unbearably tiny.

"We can hear its heartbeat? Now?" Andy asks, again. "That's amazing!"

"It's smaller than a grain of rice, but yes, it has a heart-beat." She continues to look at the screen and does something to make the images shift a little. "Aaaaaaaand . . . it's not the only one in there. See the other one? It's looking good too!"

I sit up a little on my elbows, straining to look at the screen. Andy and I look at each other with eyes bulging, unblinking. Andy starts to sway a little. "Holy . . . I mean, I'm sorry . . . What do you mean 'the other one'? The other one . . . stuck too?" He struggles for words.

"Yup! Twins! Congratulations!" she says. "So, we'll be seeing you every week now." She continues to talk very mat-ter-of-factly, but the words swirl away from me as my mind attempts to speed forward toward the end of nine months.

I lie back down, looking at the screen and then again at the ceiling. I search out the Caribbean waters for some reas-suring sign, even a glimpse of some fantastical creature or remnant of angels' wings in the skies. The sunlight glances off the impossibly blue water into my eyes. I look down at my hands. My legs. My feet. *Two* embryos. Here we are looking at them. Both of them. They both made it. We'd tried so hard for so long, and all of a sudden there are two. *They* are there with heartbeats glowing like flickering fireflies.

I put one hand down to my stomach. I cover my face with my arm. I start to laugh and weep. I have a flashback, remem-bering when I was a child. My mother and I are playing with a little baby doll and giving it a bath. I watch my mom's hands scrub the baby clean, and I do my best to mimic her hands, her worn and tired hands. She coos at the baby doll and I coo too, singing *san-toki-toki-yah*, the Korean mountain rabbit song. Mountains and waters were images that surrounded me as a child, and they would continue to mark the terrain of my life.

I had no idea that this would be the actual journey, this struggling, floundering, flailing in the waters of faithfulness . . . of God. The whole time I was questioning and wonder-ing whether I could stay faithful to God and to this dream of having a family and being a mother. The whole time I was wondering what it means for me to falter and to fall away, really it was a question of me trusting in God's faithfulness. As the little ones grew in my body, swimming and turning in those amniotic waters, I felt myself also splashing and diving deeper into the waters of God's love for me. It was a continuous baptism and affirmation of my ordination vows—remembering Whose I am, and how my belonging to God meant that, no matter what my calling, I would be surrounded by God's steadfast presence.

Vocational Clarity: Being Open to the Process

I changed jobs. We moved to the Midwest in April 2011. My husband, Andy, who is also clergy, responded to God's call to serve the First Presbyterian Church in Bloomington, Indiana, as their head of staff. I had been an associate pastor for youth and children at Presbyterian churches for more than seven years, and I now found myself serving a much smaller parish, with only two child members—my twin babies.

Upon the twins' arrival, my vocational identity shifted quite abruptly and threw me into an unfamiliar world. Instead of reading theological commentaries, I found myself scouring books on parenting and babies' development during the first year. Instead of leading devotionals for committee meetings, I was washing cloth diapers. Instead of crafting alternative worship experiences for the youth on Wednesday evenings, I was bouncing babies in chairs to help them fall asleep. Instead of writing sermons, organizing mission trips, training Sunday school teachers, and reaching out to the community, I was doing the bare minimum to survive long enough to make it to the next day when the seemingly endless cycle of feed-burp-change-play-sleep would begin again. Instead of enjoying a happy hour at the local pub, I was counting down the minutes until bedtime.

Quicker than you can gulp down a shot of tequila, I went from being a full-time pastor to being a full-time mom. More accurately and simply, I became a stay-at-home mom. I was wandering in a wilderness. Anxious. Fearful. Delirious.

Throughout most of my life, my connection to God had felt relatively straightforward. Though there were times when I felt distant from God because of certain choices or questions that felt like a struggle, I still maintained a sense of God's nearness. During my first year in seminary, I went home every Friday afternoon after the theology precept and cried into my pillow. So much was unraveling for me, everything that I had grown up trusting. But even then, even when all that was familiar was being stripped from me, I miraculously felt God expanding in my life. Even in the deepest darkness, I never felt completely forsaken.

Becoming a parent was viscerally different. Fear colored every moment. If I was driving around with the babies, at every four-way intersection I paused for much longer than necessary. Images of a huge Ford truck barreling through without stopping and t-boning my little Subaru plagued me. If I laid the babies down on the carpet, I walked on eggshells, dreading the possibility that I might accidentally step on a baby's head. If I was in the grocery store with the babies, I steered clear of anyone coughing for fear of some disease that might infect them. I became totally and completely irrational in my fear, and it paralyzed me.

I lost my bearings. The days passed in a blur. I was disoriented, existing in a sleep-deprived haze. Others had told me over and over that becoming a mother would fundamentally change me, but I had no idea of the extent of that change, nor was I prepared for it. On the one hand, it was clear that my body would never be the same again. I had residual aches from the pregnancy in the tips of my fingers from tendonitis and soreness all the way down to the tops of my feet. Even more so, I was mentally, emotionally, and spiritually numb from pure exhaustion.

Even so, I tried to continue the same rituals that had always nourished and centered me. I tried prayer and quiet times.

Sunday morning church. Devotional books. But I was listless, unfocused, and, of course, distracted by the needs of these very young and demanding creatures. Although I was no doubt head-over-heels in love with them, I was also overwhelmed with guilt about not doing—and being—enough for them, for Andy, for family and friends, and, finally, for my faith. All of it was so overwhelming that I concluded that if I couldn't give God my all, or at least what I had given in the past, then I shouldn't bother giving anything at all to God. I avoided thinking or feeling anything, and quickly I hit rock bottom.

One day, I came across Brené Brown, professor and TED Talk speaker, who spoke into my struggle:

> The only choice we really have is how we're going to respond to feeling vulnerable. And contrary to popular belief, our shields don't protect us. They simply keep us from being seen, heard, and known.
>
> If there's anything I've learned over the past decade and experienced firsthand over the last year, it's this: *Our willingness to own and engage with our vulnerability determines the depth of our courage and the clarity of our purpose.*
>
> Even if letting ourselves be seen and opening ourselves up to judgment or disappointment feels terrifying, the alternatives are worse: Choosing to feel nothing—numbing. Choosing to perfect, perform, and please our way out of vulnerability. Choosing rage, cruelty, or criticism. Choosing shame and blame. Like most of you reading this, I have some experience with all of these alternatives, and they all lead to the same thing: disengagement and disconnection.
>
> One of my favorite quotes is from theologian Howard Thurman. He writes, "Don't ask what the world needs; ask what makes you come alive, and go do it. Because what the world needs is more people who have come alive." Vulnerability is not easy, but it's the surest sign that we've come alive.[3]

This word about vulnerability was a lifesaver. After months of being constantly awake at night, and of feeling so empty and plain desperate, I sat down and finally picked up my pen—something that I used to do regularly but had put aside after the babies' arrival. The pen came alive, and the paper seemed to fill itself. I confronted my longing and all my struggles with jealousy, despair, and even anger.

> In the forced quiet, though brief, as the babies drift off to fitful sleep, I can mentally write up all manner of to-do lists or lamely scour Facebook searching for anything and everything to distract me from the inner reality.
>
> I long for where I imagine I might be in this moment—a beach, a conference, a New York City café. I am jealous of other women, pastors, writers, adventure-seekers, mothers who seem to have and do it all. I despair at the thought of doing this indefinitely, waiting around for the twins to fall asleep and stay asleep. I am angry at them for waking up, I am angry at myself for being so heartless and impatient and selfish. I am afraid that this is all there is for me now.

Embracing Brown's affirmation of brokenness and openness was an oasis of sorts, and it allowed me to see other paths for my life. My plans were waylaid, but I could still pursue God, wherever I found myself, even if it meant learning and relearning the journey. The crack that appeared in my fear and guilt was significant enough to let in what was necessary—God's grace—which allowed me to breathe in that air once again. It made me see the possibility of motherhood as an invitation to create—re-create, reinvent, redefine—my relationships, with myself, with others, and especially with God. It would compel me to new ways of experiencing God's goodness.

And then my dear friend Christine sent me a blog post called "The Desert Mothers Didn't Change Diapers. But Maybe They Should Have," written by Penny Carothers, a guest writer on Don Miller's blog *Don Miller Is*. She articulated exactly what I was feeling in terms of thinking that my spirituality, my faith life, my devotional life, my connection to God needed to be a certain way. She challenged that obligation and offered the possibility of "the sanctification of the ordinary" in these words:

> What if there really is a different way? What if God intended the hug of a child to mirror the numinous moment others achieve through meditation? What if attending to the needs and the play of children—really attending, not reading the news on my phone or folding laundry while I listen with half an ear—was a window into the spiritual? What if all I really needed to do was simply be present? After all, God calls himself a lover and a parent, and perhaps there is something to learn in embracing my life rather than trying to escape it so I can have real communion with God.
>
> It's still a little shocking, but perhaps the most spiritual thing I can do may be to embrace my life as a mother. Not a spiritual, metaphorical mother, but a snot-wiping, baby-chasing, diaper bag-toting mother. Because sometimes it's not the bible stories or the lectio divina, but the *Help!* and *thank you* that a relationship is built on.[4]

I realized that this was what I needed most: to reframe as Sabbath this whole year and whatever the future might hold for me. Sabbath was a strange concept in our home growing up. We spent all day at the church, and it was busy and full. We were constantly surrounded by people, like an extended family, with elders and deacons standing in as uncles and aunts, and as children we played hard and ate well those days. Even though the Sabbath was chaotic, it was still somehow tranquil, and I would carry this kind of contentment into adulthood.

But, with the utter chaos of having children, the times of restoration looked quite different from what I had experienced in the past—bed and breakfasts with books or a trip into New York City and museums—but it eventually nourished me in surprising ways. Vulnerability and openness—these became necessary characteristics of Sabbath, and fragility allowed me to receive God's presence. I began to approach each day drenched in God's love for me. Though the struggle had not completely dissipated, it no longer had a hold on me. I was okay with not having a job, with not having an identity outside of being "the twins' mom," with not having anything official or professional to pursue in the future right now. I was more than okay to drink from the ordinary and the everyday.

Advent arrived, and though I didn't read my usual devotional book or attend all of the worship services or even have an Advent wreath, I spent at least once a week reflecting on the lectionary text. I relished Madeleine L'Engle's short poem *After Annunciation*, which says,

> *This is the irrational season*
> *When love blooms bright and wild.*
> *Had Mary been filled with reason*
> *There'd have been no room for the child.*[5]

I played Christmas hymns on the piano. I preached one Sunday at the other local Presbyterian church, and I feasted on God's presence in a little corner of Starbucks as I listened to the David Nevue channel on Pandora, read commentaries and blogs, and wrote the sermon. But, the most sweet and savory, the most irrational, bright, and wild moments that gave me life were these:

I dressed up the babies for Christmas Eve service, and I held my baby girl in my arms as we stood to sing "Hark! The Herald Angels Sing!" and "Joy to the World!" and I could hear her voice too as she sang, "Ba-ba-ba-ba!"

I napped with my baby boy one afternoon, since he wouldn't fall asleep on his own because he was too excited about pulling himself up to stand in his crib.

I stood the babies up on the couch, and we pressed our faces against the window to watch the snow fall.

I grabbed my daughter and danced with her, and swung her around, and danced with my son and watched his face fill with glee as I threw him up in the air and caught him in my arms.

I let myself get soaked during the babies' rough-housing and squealing in the bath—a veritable cleansing for my soul each night.

Vocational Supplement: Being Courageous in the Season

Parents rarely let go of their children, so children let go of them.
They move on. They move away.
The moments that used to define them are covered by
moments of their own accomplishments.
It is not until much later, that children understand;
their stories and all their accomplishments, sit atop the stories
of their mothers and fathers, stones upon stones,
beneath the water of their lives.[6]

Parenthood is not for the faint of heart. Before Andy and I got married, we talked about having children. It was just a given that we would have children, and that when it came to that point, we would work out what our full-time careers would look like while raising them. Of course, as the old adage based on Robert Burns's poem says, "The best laid plans of mice and men often go astray."

When our babies did finally arrive to grace our lives, few words could truly describe the changes that happened to us as a couple. Gut-wrenching. Mind-numbing. Life-altering. These descriptions hardly do it justice, but they come close. Anything along the lines of military boot camp, backpacking in the wilderness, and running marathons would provide adequate language. And while there are sky-high piles of stories about the wonder and magic of becoming parents, only in recent history with the widespread availability of social media have we heard that parenting is much more than cuddling a squishy newborn, and that it is, in fact, one of the most difficult endeavors that we would enter into as a couple.

Still, neither of us would say anything less than that these children have captured our hearts.

> Each suburban wife struggles with it alone. As she made the beds, shopped for groceries, matched slipcover material, ate peanut butter sandwiches with her children, chauffeured Cub Scouts and Brownies, lay beside her husband at night—she was afraid to ask even of herself the silent question—"Is this all?"[7]

The notion of primary versus secondary breadwinner and caregiver came up when we discussed a leave of absence with both our churches. Growing up and watching my mother be the primary caregiver, I had assumed that all women were mothers, or at least destined to be mothers, and the church I grew up in gave me even more mothers. Every Korean woman was a kind of mother to us children. The whole notion of parental leave felt new as we ourselves stepped into parenthood for the first time.

Fortunately, we both had the opportunity to take maternity and paternity leaves. This parity was a blessing and a wonderful expression of how far the church has come in supporting clergy and their families. Although my previous church did not have a maternity policy technically in place, the personnel committee worked quickly and fairly to provide me with support, despite the news that our family was leaving to follow God's call to Andy to a church in Bloomington. Without this time of transition into having the twins, I'm not sure that we would have survived the first two months of their lives.

When we moved to Bloomington and after the dust settled a bit, I began to examine what it really meant to be the primary caregiver to the children. According to Wikipedia,

> A primary caregiver is the person who takes primary responsibility for someone who cannot care fully for themselves. It may be a family

> member, a trained professional or another individual. Depending on culture, there may be various members of the family engaged in care. The concept can be important in attachment theory as well as in family law, for example in guardianship and child custody.[8]

Though "primary caregiver" is a legal designation, it felt like much more. In day-to-day terms, I know that being the twins' primary caregiver means that I am the one who will be the most present with the children on a regular basis. When they were little, this meant feeding and changing them, helping them sleep, and playing with them. It also meant that I would be "on" constantly. The hours started to bleed into each other, so that it really didn't matter if it was day or night—only how many hours until their next nap. I remember snoozing on the couch early one Sunday morning while the twins slept in their bouncy seats. Andy had come down to get ready to go to church. It felt as if he had become quite unaware of the noise he was making, slamming all the cabinet doors shut. I woke up, the babies stirred and started to fuss, and I hissed in my loudest quiet voice, "PLEASE DO NOT SLAM THE CABINET DOORS! The babies just fell asleep, and this is all I wanted from them, and they are finally asleep, and you woke all of us up, and . . . I hate my life!"

Needless to say, Andy was rattled. He left for work pretty quickly, and I sat in the dark, bouncing the chairs, wondering how I had gotten to this point. Is this what I signed up for when I became a parent?

"Twenty-four/seven. . . . Once you sign on to be a mother, that's the only shift they offer."[9]

If I was the twins' primary caregiver, did that mean that this would be my only job? My only vocation? Would I carry the bulk of this work? Somehow it became more than work and more like a fundamental change in my being. Becoming a parent was viscerally different from anything else. I was madly in love with these babies. I stared at them every possible second. I constantly held their little hands, looking at tiny fingers that couldn't possibly one day hold mine back. I wanted to freeze them in this moment forever so they wouldn't have to face peer pressure, body image issues, and stupid kids breaking their hearts. I believed that every single movement and facial twitch was an expression of the Divine.

I had to let go of set job descriptions. Some of the struggle was about watching Andy go off to work every day and feeling only loss—that is, loss of value and worth, loss of equality. I could only think of my mother, who was always a homemaker and then eventually became a second-career pastor's wife when my father became a pastor late in life. The hierarchy didn't change much in their relationship, and they became even more entrenched in their roles because of this new job. But, any hierarchy in these roles is tricky and, in many ways, unhelpful and unnecessary. For some, perhaps, this structure is comforting, but I needed to see that I still possessed some agency.

Bottom line: we learned to share the load in a way that allows for fluidity in our roles. Most mornings Andy unloads the dishwasher and starts breakfast for the twins. I usually take on the bath at night. But this can change too. Sometimes there are meetings, or last-minute pastoral visitations, or college student gatherings. So we adjust and work it out. Flexibility is the new norm, and communication nurtures and maintains it. There is simply no way to have a neat blueprint for who is going to do or give up what at all times to make this family life sustainable. But, I had to speak up, and I had to be willing to do and say what was necessary for us to survive each day.

Quoting Daniel Bell, Bonnie J. Miller-McLemore observes, "'The recovery of sacrifice entails seeing it as a central practice in a cycle of gift-exchange, in which giving does not result in loss but rather nurtures communion, mutuality, and interdependence.' Sacrifice is not the height and epitome of love. Sacrifice stands in service of mutuality."[10] This perspective on sacrifice helped me to reframe my vocation in such a way that I see that I was not losing or lacking, but that I am part of something much bigger. To compare or compete, to keep track of or quantify the daily sacrifices only cuts away at the roots that tie us together. Because essentially, we both make sacrifices.

In a weird way, both my husband and I are primary caregivers. Ayelet Waldman states:

> Even if I'm setting myself up for failure, I think it's worth trying to be a mother who delights in who her children are, in their knock-knock jokes and earnest questions. A mother who spends less time obsessing about what will happen, or what has happened, and more time reveling in what is. A mother who doesn't fret over failings and slights, who realizes her worries and anxieties are just thoughts, the continuous chattering and judgment of a too busy mind. A mother who doesn't worry so much about being bad or good but just recognizes that she's both, and neither. A mother who does her best, and for whom that is good enough, even if, in the end, her best turns out to be, simply, not bad.[11]

Becoming a pastor and then a parent is an ego-killer. I can still hear my parents' voices in my ear—*gohsang hae*—as they remind me that to struggle and suffer is important for building character. In my life things humble me time and time again. As a pastor, my days felt full of minute and impossible decisions, and constant second-guessing. *Should I have . . . ? Would I have . . . ? What if . . . ?* This was the most obvious overlap in motherhood and ministry. In caring for the children, I constantly wonder whether I should be doing something else, whether it be earning more income or doing more crafts with them.

Thankfully, I did not have to go this alone.

One of the reasons we made the decision to follow God's call to Bloomington for Andy's position was the desire to be in church together on Sunday mornings with our children. We had never really experienced this at all, and having children made sharing a community on Sundays much more urgent to us. What I did not anticipate at all was how trying it would be for me to sit in the pews with them alone Sunday after Sunday while Andy worked and led worship. Although the church community surrounded us with much love and encouragement, it was still a lonely endeavor. What complicated it even more was constantly facing in Andy's presence in the pulpit what I had given up: pastoral identity, church community, and an important livelihood.

Of course, we had countless conversations about my struggle to accept the reality that I could not have it all. I knew that I wanted to stay at home with the children for at least the first year. I knew that moving to Bloomington would mean likely not being called to a church. I knew that eventually I would want to work again in some capacity.

I spent the middle-of-the-night hours checking who else was up on Facebook, scouring parenting blogs, and writing e-mails to mom-friends lamenting this season of our lives and asking every possible question about child development and care. One e-mail response still sticks with me now. When my mind finally turned from the children to Andy, I mentioned in passing my worry about how having children would impact our marriage, and the feeling that we were two ships passing in the night, and that the only time we would interact would be to lob cannonballs at each other from our own decks. It felt like we fought more than we talked or listened to each other.

This friend wrote back a number of little nuggets, including this one: "Don't worry about the marriage right now." This caught me off guard. I thought, *We are on the verge of killing each other most days, or we are too tired to say or do anything at all. Is it a good idea to not worry about it?*

However, what my friend was reminding me was that parenting young children is a season, just one season of our lives. It's temporary and prone to change, much like anything and everything else in our lives. She was confident that my husband and I had a strong relationship and would get through the difficult times, and that what we should do now was focus on day-to-day survival—the children's survival, our dog's survival, and our own survival. There would be time for marriage later. This was freeing and helped ease my anxiety.

She was right. When we started to lean into the routine of naps, diapers, and meals, or Andy's workweeks and meeting schedules, and surrendered to the constant reality of interruptions, it helped us to be open to other ways of connecting with each other again. We would watch episodes of shows that were new to us after the twins went down for the night. Instead of date nights we had breakfasts, and we even celebrated an anniversary at a favorite restaurant for brunch. We were too tired for date nights anyway, but when we were able to leave the twins for more than two hours, many church members volunteered to be with them so that we could go out for the occasional dinner or drink. We took advantage of the "Kids' Night In" once a month so that we could grab a quick, early supper. And our being together made more and more sense, and we remembered not only how much we love each other, but also how much we enjoy each other.

Even so, I vacillated between bucking against cultural pressures to be the perfect and willing stay-at-home mom and embracing this as an opportunity to experience and live into greater faithfulness. I tried more to frame this as the latter. There were countless occasions for learning about patience, kindness, and gentleness, which are virtues that I needed to cultivate in my life—not just with the children, but even more so with Andy. I was living and learning what it means not to fixate over every little detail and task. To see how much the sarcastic words that I said over and over again were detrimental to both of us. To see how little acts of intentional generosity went a long way. To see how this whole life together is made all the more better with honesty and hope—and with each other.

The journey through this season of parenthood continues to shape me not only me as a mother or pastor, but also as a spouse and as a human being. I continue in my development as a minister even though I am without a church that I serve each week. But, with the addition of another child, I have three parishioners that need me right now, four including the dog, five including Andy. My definition of ministry has become broader because of my job as a parent. I continue to be thankful for the ways my parents modeled parenthood for me faithfully, and I hope that I will live into it my own way too.

NOTES

1. Andrew Solomon, *Far from the Tree: Parents, Children, and the Search for Identity* (New York: Scribner, 2012), chapter 1, paragraph 16 (Kindle edition).
2. Ibid., chapter 1, paragraph 43.
3. Brené Brown, "The Power of Vulnerability," *Huffington Post*, December 15, 2011 (http://www.huffingtonpost.com/2011/12/15/brene-brown-vulnerability_n_1150976.html).
4. Penny Carothers, "The Desert Mothers Didn't Change Diapers. But Maybe They Should Have" (http://storylineblog.com/2011/10/26/the-desert-mothers-didnt-change-diapers-but-maybe-they-should-have/).
5. Madeleine Engle, *The Ordering of Love: The New and Collected Poems of Madeleine L'Engle* (Colorado Springs, CO: Shaw Books, 2005), 153.
6. Paulo Coelho, quoted in Mitch Albom, *The Five People You Meet in Heaven* (New York: Hyperion, 2003), 128.
7. Betty Friedan, *The Feminine Mystique*, 50th anniversary edition (New York: W. W. Norton, 2013), 6.
8. Wikipedia, "Caregiver" (http://en.wikipedia.org/wiki/Caregiver).
9. Jodi Picoult, *My Sister's Keeper: A Novel* (New York: Washington Square Press, 2004), 174.
10. Bonnie J. Miller-McLemore, *In the Midst of Chaos: Caring for Children as Spiritual Practice* (San Francisco: Jossey-Bass, 2009), chapter 5, section "Salvaging Sacrifice" (Kindle edition).
11. Ayelet Waldman, *Bad Mother: A Chronicle of Maternal Crimes, Minor Calamities, and Occasional Moments of Grace* (New York: Doubleday, 2009), 207–8.

2

"Do You Speak English?"

Racial Discrimination and Being the "Perpetual Foreigner"

GRACE JI-SUN KIM

I speak fluent English, conversational Korean, and textbook French. I am proud to be trilingual, and I always encourage my children to speak Korean with me. They never do. I do my best to speak to them in Korean, unless I am disciplining them. Then, only English comes out of my mouth.

We live in a multilingual world; it is wonderful to hear different languages. However, in the small corner of the world where I live, it is difficult to hear a language other than English.

Last spring, I was in and out of the hospital several times over the span of two months. Each time I entered the hospital the first thing the doctor would ask me was "Do you speak English?" It is a simple question, and perhaps I should not have become so upset. However, if one doctor after another and one nurse after another keeps asking me, "Do you speak English?" it gets to be quite annoying. I would love to scream back, "Of course I speak English!" But I try to remain calm, and I sheepishly answer, "Yes."

On one level, I realize that I should not be so annoyed and offended. Perhaps the hospital has a protocol specifying that staff members need to figure out if a person is ethnic and whether he or she can speak English. Still, every time a doctor asks me this question, I wonder if they ask a white, European American patient the same thing.

Minorities are always asked to define themselves or are identified with some form of adjective, while white, European Americans are never asked to define themselves. This actually allows the dominant, kyriarchical system to keep its presumptions of "normativity," while forcing those who do not fit that category to continually identify themselves. Elisabeth Schüssler Fiorenza utilizes "kyriarchy" to describe all the forms of dominating hierarchies, such as sexism, racism, and homophobia, which subordinate a group or individuals.[1] The word "kyriarchy" comes from the Greek words *kyrios*, which means "lord," and *archō*, which means "to rule." Kyriarchy becomes a system that is built upon oppression and subjugation. It hurts people and damages them. These unjust systems become interrelated and work toward internalizing and institutionalizing subordination and oppression against certain groups of people.

Among the various systemic forms of oppression, many come into play to describe who I am. For example, I am never viewed or understood as simply a "woman," but I am viewed and defined as an "Asian American woman." As a result, I am continually viewed as inferior to white women and understood as the other. My identity becomes tied to my physical body in ways that are never applied to those in power or those making rules.

During one hospital visit I spoke with a nurse for about five minutes, when she suddenly asked, "Is English your preferred language?" And I wondered what prompted her to ask me that question after talking with me for five minutes. Did I look confused? Further, would she ask white patients the same question?

If everyone were asked, "Is English your preferred language of communication?" then there would be no issue. I wish everyone were asked that question by default. That would make white Americans more aware of their situation because they would find the question absurd.

I wonder what hospitals do if a person answers, "No, I do not speak English." Do hospitals train staff to be multilingual, or do they use such a response as an excuse to talk down to patients? There are so many issues of power and privilege wrapped up in such a question!

The question of whether I speak English may be totally innocent. Good intentions may lie behind it. But, when I am consistently asked about my ability to speak English, it raises questions for me: Who am I in my community? How do the people who are providing my care see me?

I look Asian, and therefore to many in my community I will constantly be viewed as a foreigner who lives in their midst. The question of whether I speak English leads me to wonder if, in the eyes of members of the dominant culture, I will ever truly belong. Will I be accepted for who I am? Or will I be forever seen, and treated, as an outsider?

Foreigners have traditionally been viewed with suspicion, scapegoated, and blamed as a source of many problems. For example, the foreign women in the book of Ezra (Ezra 10) were told to leave their husbands, children, and families. The Book of Ezra contains a crucial part of Israelite history which begins with the return of the exiles. Ezra is the only biblical book that attempts to give a history of the postexilic era,[2] and thus it becomes a very important book as it gives us information of some of the difficulties, struggles, and hardships that the returnees and the ones who never left had to deal and struggle with. Ezra 9 records the community leaders' choice to identify the reinstated community of Israel through a rigid, fundamental interpretation of ancient Scripture (see Deuteronomy 7:1-6).

It is a difficult text to read and interpret, especially for those who seek fairness and justice. In an attempt to honor the ancient edicts against intermarriage that were set down when the Israelites first entered the Promised Land generations earlier, Ezra deplored the presence of foreign wives and mixed offspring as defiling the purity of God's chosen people. With the support of Jerusalem's leaders, the foreign wives were told to leave. This choice resulted in foreign wives being expelled from the land, a decision that must have torn the very fabric of the exiled community apart. The generational devastation this must have caused cannot be fully understood or described. Yet, this decision was condoned—and even praised as an act of faithfulness—by the nation's religious leaders. The foreign women were thrown out of the community. Even the term *foreigner* was a misnomer as some of these "foreigners" were those who had remained in the land until the ones living in exile in a foreign country returned.

These outcast and marginalized women of Ezra's day bring to mind other women and children who feel excluded, unwelcomed, and abandoned even now based solely on their racial or ethnic identity. In our present world there are many communities and even countries trying to rebuild their lives in the shadow of postcolonialism, identity loss, migrations, and exile. Ezra is relevant to these pertinent issues of our time, not as a pattern to be duplicated, but as a source of discussion to help us rebuild broken communities. Our nations have become divided with widely diverging views on immigration, women, people of color, and much more. The issues raised in the writings of Ezra provide a focusing lens through which discussion aimed at tearing down divisive walls and rebuilding broken communities can begin.

How then to understand the compulsion in Ezra 9–10 to expel defenseless women and children as impure, abandoning them to an unknown fate? This may be an outcome of Ezra-Nehemiah's association of the feminine with the unclean (an association exceeding that of Leviticus). This signifies an irreparable trauma at the core of Judean identity, a trauma that the text both records and tries unsuccessfully to repress. In sociologist Julia Kristeva's perspective, the subjectivity of individuals and of communities alike is always divided against itself. Ezra-Nehemiah is a tragic narrative of a fragile, emerging Judean subjectivity. The community is at odds with itself, and it must wrench itself apart in order to constitute itself. But in this struggle the purity strictures fall disproportionately on the women.[3] This disproportionality is due to society's knee-jerk ability to portray the women as the other and therefore subordinate and subjugate them. It happens so easily within the community in Ezra, and if we are not vigilant, it can also happen within our communities today.

The decision of the Israelite leaders prompts us to examine how we treat those whom we call foreigners. The United States of America is a land of immigrants, and God calls us to welcome the strangers and to love our neighbors as ourselves. Do our neighbors only include those whom we like or those who look like us? If this is the way we categorize neighbors, it will lead to problematic decisions as we try to live in harmony with a land of immigrants and foreigners.

Within our present context, foreigners are often blamed for troubles that occur in society. For example, when workers at Chrysler were losing their jobs in the late 1970s and early 1980s due to the rapidly increasing market share of Japanese automakers, many of them blamed Japanese Americans for it. Ronald Ebens and Michael Nitz, two white men who were angry because they believed that the Japanese were taking their jobs, beat Vincent Chin with a baseball bat, mistakenly thinking that he was Japanese American, when actually he was Chinese American. Chin died four days later.

I am viewed as a foreigner, and I often feel a similar tension with and discrimination from those I encounter. Some find it difficult to welcome me fully into the circle due to their (usually) unconscious suspicions of me, which flow from their view of me as an outsider. Viewed as a foreigner, I become an easy target and a scapegoat when blame must be assigned. I remember often being blamed for something that I did not do. Asian American woman are often stereotyped as quiet, subservient, and subordinate women. If I act outside of this stereotypical norm, I become a target and viewed as a 'bad' person. For example, if I speak up and point out wrongful acts that are happening, I often get accused for the wrongful acts rather than the perpetrators themselves. Too often, I am blamed for things for which my white friends or acquaintances would never be blamed. This is easily done as I am viewed as a foreigner and are often scapegoated for others' problems.

If I point out such discrimination to my friends, they sometimes label me as a troublemaker. If I keep the experience to myself, they think, "She never mentions any, so there must be no discrimination." I'm in a no-win situation.

As I think about the simple but disturbing question, "Do you speak English?" I wonder how many more times I will be asked that question again. I will be asked again and again, as I am continually viewed as the other and the foreigner. I will be perceived as a person who does not belong in this country. The same is true of my children, and so my heart aches when I imagine how many times they will be asked that same question.

Therefore, to move forward, we must ask ourselves how our churches and North American society can work together to attend to the fact that bodies marked by "foreignness" are often hurting, as foreign bodies are targets of racism. Our Asian physical characteristics will continue to mark us as foreigners, and in turn we are treated as such.

God is clear on how we are expected to treat the foreigner: "When an alien resides with you in your land, you shall not oppress the alien. The alien who resides with you shall be to you as the citizen among you; you shall love the alien as yourself, for you were aliens in the land of Egypt: I am the LORD your God" (Leviticus 19:33-34). As Christians, we must seek ways to welcome the foreigner and those who are different from us. Christ loved all people regardless of physical attributes, social status, gender, and so on (Matthew 25:34-40). We must do likewise. This can be achieved as we begin with a critical reevaluation of how systems of power and privilege persistently mark certain people in small ways that have a large impact. Kyriarchical systems that subordinate others need to be questioned, examined, challenged, and eliminated. Only by attending to the daily existence of being marked as "foreign" or "other" can we provide firm ground for our larger goals of ending systemic racism.

NOTES

1. For further discussion, see Elisabeth Schüssler Fiorenza, *But She Said: Feminist Practices of Biblical Interpretation* (Boston: Beacon Press, 1993).

2. Tamara Cohn Eskenazi, "Ezra-Nehemiah" in *The Women's Bible Commentary*, edited by Carol A. Newsom & Sharon H. Ringe (Louisville: Westminster/John Knox Press, 1992), 116.

3. Harold C. Washington, "Israel's Holy Seed and the Foreign Women of Ezra-Nehemiah: A Kristevan Reading," *Biblical Interpretation* 11,3/4(2003):428, 429.

3

"Go Somewhere Else"

CHRISTINE J. HONG

The words seared my spirit: "Go somewhere else." I left the senior minister's office with an ache at the back of my neck and hot tears welling up in the corners of my eyes. I walked away as quickly as I could, a fake smile on my face to distract other people from the weep-fest that was about to go down.

Remembering the Call

Bright-eyed and bushy-tailed, fresh from seminary, I decided that I wanted to seek a ministry placement at a Korean American congregation. I felt called back to my context, the Korean American immigrant church that had nurtured and challenged me.

Gender had been an issue in the past. When discerning my call during my college years, I approached mentors and church leaders with hopes of affirmation. Instead, I heard, "You aren't practical enough for ministry" or "Isn't what you really feel a call to be a pastor's wife?" Only later did I realize being "practical" meant being male. I also came to wonder how many pastors' wives had felt a call to ordained ministry but had settled for marrying a pastor instead of becoming a pastor themselves.

Despite the rough start, however, I always felt connected to my Korean American roots. The community mattered to me, and I wanted back in.

The interviews were bizarre. They usually started with "So, how old are you anyway?" or "Are your parents okay with this?" Some congregations asked if I could play the piano, if I liked children, or if I planned on getting married any time in the near future. When I admitted that I was not that great with children and they made me nervous, and that secretly I was afraid I might drop them, the conversations ended abruptly. When I asked why they posed these questions, the response was, "Well, women follow their husbands when they get married, so you wouldn't stay here long." One interview ended with an elderly Korean American pastor giving me a paternalistic pat on my rear end as I left his office. He handed me a hundred dollar bill, saying, "Go have something good to eat."

The worst was when one interviewer asked if I had any ambitions to become a senior minister some day. Initially, I thought that this was a prodding encouragement, as if to say that I *should* be thinking about such things. However, I realized that he was checking to see if I would fall in line. He was checking to see if I would try to reach beyond the boundaries set for me.

Through it all, humiliating and strange as it was, I felt it: the call that obscure but firm feeling that, even with the odds stacked against me, the Spirit would bring me together with the right congregation and the right people.

A Conditional Call

"We know that you are looking for an ordained and installed position, but we are not ready for something like that." After a long series of interviews, a congregation made me an offer, but it was conditional. Even though I had passed my ordination exams and been declared "ready to receive a call" by the presbytery, it was becoming increasingly evident that this did not mean much to the people I hoped to impress. The congregation's offer was a probationary one. I had one year to prove that I could do this job, fulfill this call as a woman, and fulfill it as a woman who, in their eyes, was too young. If the year passed without incident, they would ordain me. I accepted.

The Little Things

I struggled feverishly that year. Little things hurt the most. There was the time I was not allowed to drive the church van; I had to find a man to drive the youth group around. There was the time I literally had my hand slapped because I gave a blessing at the end of a youth service that looked far too much like a benediction. There was the time I was told to cut my hair shorter, wear less makeup, and dress more modestly. The latter hurt the most because it came from a group of well-meaning women who claimed they saw me as a daughter and they would not want their daughter running around that way. It shamed and angered me because I thought about how my own mother would feel if she heard those kinds of statements about her daughter.

However, there were wonderful moments too. Those moments when girls told me in confidence that they felt they were called to ministry, or when every seat and corner of my office was occupied by high school students eating chips and telling funny stories. There was the gift of being present when God moved in wonderful and powerful ways among our youth. There were those moments of seeing youth become vulnerable and share their stories of brokenness and of mending and being embraced by their church family. Most memorably, there was the laughter, the glorious laughter that still rings merrily in my ears.

Hammers and Healing

Despite the rough patches, the year went by quickly and without any major incidents, surprising me more than anyone else. Eagerly, I approached my session and the senior minister with my ordination plans in hand. Another Korean clergywoman from our church was seeking ordination that year too. This solidarity was encouraging and like balm for an open wound. However, when we approached the senior minister he seemed aggravated. I shared my wish for a modest ordination service with friends, family, and congregants. He countered with a suggestion for the two of us to share a single twenty-minute ordination service, done "quietly" on a day when there would not be too many people in town.

An ordination service that would be done "quietly" and jointly did not feel right, at least not to me. Each of us wanted to mark our ordination day with something that felt personal and sacred to us. On top of this, his response made me feel like my ordination, which was supposed to be a shared moment of joy and celebration between my church family and myself, was a burden to the congregation, and that my desire to celebrate it was the ultimate in selfish requests.

At that moment, I began to doubt myself. I went to that place in my mind where hides the filial daughter, the part of myself who has learned to consider herself last in the patriarchal hierarchy. Was I asking for too much? I did not want to hurt the people alongside whom I served. I did not want to pressure them into doing something that they did not want to do. Was it not enough that a Korean American congregation was willing to accept me and ordain me at the end of that long year? Was I behaving like some sort of diva with my ordination plan?

Then the realization hit me: I was not asking for a band, for fireworks, or for anything that glittered. I was asking for my mother and grandmother, the spiritual matriarchs of my family, to place my robe around me for the first time. I was asking for my teachers and mentors from seminary to charge me for the ministry ahead. I was asking for my friends and my fellow Korean American clergywomen to shout joyfully with me. I was asking for my youth group to lead worship and for the congregation to see how gifted and brilliant their children were. I wanted to be in the midst of a cloud of witnesses.

My ordination had been hard-won. It had started with a journey to seminary that at first did not have the acceptance of my family, my church, my pastor, or my spiritual mentors. However, it ended with the love and support of those who at first had feared and doubted me. It continued to be about the community that had carried me and still carries me on their shoulders. I wanted to honor them and the road that we had traveled together faithfully. I was not satisfied with a quiet and joint ordination service. I shared this dissatisfaction, and the response I heard was this: "Go somewhere else!" He said, "If you want to make this a show, go somewhere else. Rent out a gym or a room somewhere, but don't invite anyone from the church. No one will come."

Those words hit me like a hammer. I barely made it back to my office before the tears started falling. Was a pastor's first call always like this—humiliating, belittling, frightening? Did this response come because I was a woman and I did not fit into the preconceived mold of Korean American femininity? Did my male counterparts go through this? Maybe it was normal.

I decided to let it go. One morning, one of our high school students and her mother came bursting through the church office door. The two had heard that I was seeking ordination, but they were puzzled because they had not heard of any plans yet—no place, date, or time set. "We're running out of time," they said. "We need to get started! How about flowers? I can do all the flowers. Don't worry. I have someone who will do the food. What else can we do?"

Those words were an offering and a healing gift. I felt my spirit cradled.

Coming Home to Community

Like a forceful tidal wave, the families, and especially the women, of the congregation bought any dissenters around through their enthusiasm and support. The service came together beautifully. Old friends and family members met my new friends and my church family. Colleagues helped put together invitations; youth put on their best to lead everyone in worship; a mentor and spiritual advisor gave me the charge to live boldly and prophetically. Deacons prepared food and flowers; my mother and grandmother placed vestments over my shoulders; my friends and I locked eyes as I gave my first benediction; and ultimately the senior minister laid his hands on me in ordination, alongside other colleagues in ministry, affirming my call to this place and time. My community had ordained me, and to the relief of some skeptics, the church did not go up in flames, a sinkhole did not appear in the sanctuary floor to swallow me up, and I did not suddenly grow horns. I no longer needed to "go somewhere else." I was home.

4

The Transformative Power of Communion

YENA K. HWANG

The first time I ever witnessed Communion being shared was at Hoo Am Catholic Church in Seoul, Korea. I was eight years old. The sunlight coming in through the stained-glass windows made a kaleidoscope of colors dance on the white lace head coverings and faces of the Eucharist recipients. It was my first worship experience in a church, and I was mesmerized by the mystery of the ritual being carried out before me. I watched with curiosity as people walked up to the altar rail and kneeled before the priest, who placed a communion wafer on their tongues. They bowed with their hands together in prayer and then made the sign of the cross before returning to their seats. I had no clue what was going on, but I felt as if I were missing out on something magical and important. I was so envious. I wanted to be part of that special group of folks receiving the bread of heaven.

Fast-forward eight years. By this time, our family had moved to the United States. We were active members of a Korean PC(USA) church. I was sixteen years old, and I was excited to receive baptism. With excitement I had memorized the essential creeds, the Ten Commandments, and whatever else was required to receive the sacrament. I thought, *I will finally taste the bread of heaven.* Our church sometimes used flat wafers and sometimes used white bread cut up into small cubes for the said bread of heaven. Elders served Communion with utmost reverence to those who were baptized and confirmed, to those who were truly penitent in heart, and to those who were deemed worthy. Communion was not celebrated regularly, as it was a solemn and important act, only to be shared on special occasions such as Easter and Christmas.

Imagine my disappointment when I finally received one of those cardboard-like wafers. Not only did it not taste like anything, but also I did not feel anything during the ritual of Communion. I did not see angels, hear heavenly music, or feel the invasion of the Holy Ghost. It turned out to be a good thing that our church celebrated Communion only three or four times a year.

Fast-forward fourteen more years. I was thirty years old and going back to graduate school for a Master of Arts in Marriage and Family Therapy (MAMFT) at Louisville Presbyterian Theological Seminary (LPTS) in Kentucky. During the orientation weekend, I met a young woman who was entering into the Master of Divinity program. Although we were going to be in two different programs, all the first-year students were scheduled to engage in "getting to know you" kinds of activities together. In one of our sessions I was paired with her, and we shared some basic personal information. We shared where we had lived prior to coming to Louisville, what schools we had attended, and our family backgrounds. I noticed a gold band on her left ring finger and asked, "So, are you married?" She had been very articulate up to this point, but she began to stumble over her words. "Well, no . . . but I have someone. . . ." She became visibly flustered, and I felt her discomfort, and we just left it at that.

The next day, she came up to me and explained the reason behind her difficulties with my question. She is gay. She wears a wedding band because she has been with her partner for ten years, and they are as committed to each other as any other married couple. She hesitated to share her relationship status with me not knowing if I was a "friend" or a "foe" and not knowing where I stood on the issue. I don't recall what I said in response, but I do remember feeling confused.

I had been living under a rock, insulated by the Korean American community that did not want to deal with issues related to homosexuality. Homosexuality was not something that needed to be studied or discussed, my community said, because "the Bible is clear on this subject." Period.

Even as a Master of Divinity student at Princeton Seminary, I had not known what to make of the issue. There were diverse theological perspectives on this issue on campus, as with anything else. During my senior year the faculty of Princeton Seminary had published a book dealing with this very issue titled *Homosexuality and Christian Community.* I thought that I would get a clear answer through that book. I didn't. Since this was not a pressing matter for me personally, I didn't give it much more thought until I encountered my new friend at Louisville Seminary. All of sudden, this became an important issue that I needed to figure out. I needed to know what to make of this new friend who loved the Lord, loved the church, and loved the people of God, and was preparing to spend her life sharing that love through her ministry.

There was much going on those early weeks of my first semester at LPTS. The reason for the recent resignation of the president of the seminary was revealed: sexual misconduct and abuse. Shortly thereafter and a week before classes were to begin, news of the resignation of the director of the MAMFT program was announced: she had been one of the victims. This was disturbing news. The pain was palpable on campus. Although I was new to the school, I felt the sting and pain of betrayal. On top of all of that, I was confused about what the correct biblical understanding of homosexuality was. I sought comfort and solace through chapel services.

It was still in the first month of the academic year. It was a Communion Friday. I don't know who led the worship or who preached that day. I just remember sitting in the pews looking around at those who had gathered to worship. There were students, professors, faculty members, supporting staff members, groundskeepers—a fairly diverse group of people, all gathered for worship. Then it was time for Communion. Muffled sounds of people walking down the aisle toward the Communion table caught my attention. Then the faces of the people caught my attention, one of which was my new friend's face. Then I had my answer. I received the Communion elements—bread from heaven, cup of the new covenant—and my eyes were opened.

We are all children of God. We are all broken people, in one form or another, who have experienced God's grace and mercy. We are people made whole by Jesus' body, broken for us, and Jesus' blood, spilled for us. It was through that Communion service that I heard the voice of God saying that we are loved, all of us, equally. There was no distinction between the highly educated professor and the first-year student, between the person who is straight and the person who is gay, between those who had sinned and those who had been sinned against, and between the students who walked the campus grounds and the laborers who tended the grounds. In God's eyes, we are all precious beloved children—period. There was no confusion. There was no doubt. It was a transformative moment.

Jesus commanded us to have table fellowship in remembrance of him—his teachings, his vision, his mission, his heart for all people, his pursuit of justice and truth. For so many years I was going through the motions of Communion without truly experiencing communion. Communion had become for me a ritualistic practice, void of transformative power—until that day, the day that I repented. I went and sought out my friend and thanked her for her courage to speak honestly with me. I cannot forget what that moment of clarity felt like for me. My eyes, ears, and heart opened up to receive God's truth, in broken pieces of bread dipped in wine. Since then, I have not forgotten the transformative power in the act of breaking bread and sharing the cup.

Every time I participate in Communion now, whether at the local congregation or at presbytery or at a retreat, I pray that the words of institution, the prayers, and the elements of bread and wine will do their mysterious work. I pray that the power of the Holy that transforms those earthly elements into heavenly elements will transform us from secular beings into holy beings, worthy to be called ambassadors for Christ, heirs with Christ, and beloved children of God.

PART II

Korean American Theology

5

The Urgent Need for an Ethic of Resistance in Korea

NAYOUNG HA

Dietrich Bonhoeffer and I share a few core things in common: both of us were international students studying in the United States; we studied at prominent seminaries (Union Theological Seminary, McCormick Theological Seminary); we had life-transforming experiences through encountering black scholars and the black church (W. E. B. Du Bois, Abyssinian Baptist Church, James Cone, Delores Williams, Linda Thomas, and Trinity United Church of Christ); and we were affiliated with a Lutheran denominational institution (Lutheran pastor, PhD student at Lutheran School of Theology at Chicago). I also discovered that we have a significant difference (besides those of gender, race, and class). Bonhoeffer finished his postgraduate study in New York in two years and then went back to Germany and lived out what he had learned from the Harlem Renaissance and the Black Christ. I, on the other hand, have been studying in Chicago for my PhD for about ten years, have not yet finished my degree, cannot go back to Korea yet, and therefore cannot live out what I have learned.

It is shameful, but I feel that I can justify putting off my theological action and practice until after I finish my studies and return to Korea. At least I thought I could do so. Then I read Reggie Williams's article "Dietrich Bonhoeffer, the Harlem Renaissance, and the Black Christ,"[1] and I realized that unlike me, Bonhoeffer never postponed acting out his theology in response to what he had learned and experienced as an international student at Union Theological Seminary in New York.

According to Williams, Bonhoeffer continued to write and reflect upon himself, his theology, and his theological context of German Christianity in light of his encounter with racial discrimination and segregation in the United States. I imagine that it was because of this continued engagement that he was led to the painful but transformative theological realization that the White Racist Christ in the United States was not very different from the Aryan Nazi Christ in Germany, and that white racist American Christians did not look very different from himself. This led him to change. He realized that in order to follow Christ hidden in the suffering of outcasts, the first thing that he had to deny and resist was the Christ with whom he had become familiar and comfortable.

This theological reflection is my attempt to begin to do such theological practice by reflecting critically upon myself, my dominant ideology, and Christianity in South Korea by asking myself these questions:

- Which Christ have the majority of Christians been taught, believed in, and grown comfortable with?
- Through which Christ have privileged groups sustained their power and supported oppressive structures in the church and society?
- Who are the most oppressed outcasts in the South Korean context?
- In order to be in solidarity with outcasts and Christ hidden in suffering, which Christ should I (or we, meaning Korean Christians) resist?

This chapter insists on the urgent need for an ethic of resistance against the dominant Christ, which operates as an ideology of sociopolitics serving the status quo in South Korea. By examining the issues around the legislation of an antidiscrimination bill, I argue that children and members of multicultural families, LGBTQI[2] people, and people who operate on the politically radical left are the outcasts who are exposed to open discrimination and violence in their everyday life in Korea. Acts of discrimination based on race or ethnicity, skin color, gender identity or sexual orientation, ideological/political orientation, and educational background in Korea have been publicly claimed as a freedom to the rights of expression, religion, and business activity by politically conservative people, the majority conservative Christians, and large corporations. I believe that in order to be in solidarity with outcasts in Korea, Korean Christians must resist a white racist, homophobic, and politically Religious Right Christ.

Resistance against the White Racist Christ

Korea is a multicultural, multiethnic, and multiracial nation. Approximately 1,500,000 foreign residents and 400,000 multicultural families live in Korea. Roughly one in ten marriages in Korea is a multicultural marriage, and in rural areas this rate increases to 50 percent. On a daily basis Koreans bully and discriminate against children in multicultural families and their non-Korean parents, spurred by strong ethnocentrism and racism. The darker your skin, the worse you are treated.[3] Korean Christians urgently need to resist the White Racist Christ within us in order to fight against racism and ethnocentrism in the society and to walk with the racially and ethnically marginalized.

The ideology of ethnocentrism, which is deeply rooted in the history of South Korea and in Korean people's minds, has joined with the ideology of white supremacy in the Christian modernization process since the 1880s. White American missionaries came to Korea, built churches and schools, and taught Koreans about their white slave owner, Christ. Korean men and women who were evangelized, educated, modernized, and Westernized by American whites became the leaders of every sector of Korean society, and they have been great followers and supporters of white America. Korean churches send more than 20,000 missionaries to some 200 countries around the world every year, and they do their best to spread the good news of the white Jesus whom they received from white American missionaries.

When Korean McCormick Theological Seminary alumna Hyeyoung Lee wanted to marry white American McCormick alumnus Kurt Esslinger, her conservative evangelical Presbyterian pastor father was not happy about her international marriage. However, after meeting Kurt in person, her father loved him and allowed the marriage because he thought that Kurt looked like Jesus—blue-eyed, shoulder-length red hair.

In her song "Black Happiness," female hip-hop singer and rapper Yoon Mi-rae (Tasha) plainly and fiercely describes her experience of and struggle against racial discrimination as a multicultural kid in South Korea. She raps:

> My skin was really black when I was younger / People would point their fingers at my mommy / My poppy's a black, U.S. military, people are whispering under their breath / Again like this and that / There were always tears welling up in my eyes / Even though I was young, I could see my mother's sadness / Feeling as if everything was my fault / Every day I'd wash my face more than twenty times / I melt the white soap in my tears / Inside I resent my black skin, why oh why / Is the world judging me / Every time I start to hate the world, I close both my eyes real tight / I place my soul in the music my father gives me as a present / Turning up the volume, I fly higher and higher.

Later in the song she describes the situation when she was on the stage: "They ask me to wear white makeup to mask up my face / My mother's bloodline is ok, but my father's not."[4]

There are countless such incidents. In 2011 Ku Su-jin, a naturalized Korean from Uzbekistan, held a news conference in Changwon, South Gyeongsang province, saying that a sauna owner denied her entrance because of her different skin color. Jeon ThiHien, a naturalized Korean from Vietnam, says that Koreans treat white people well but ignore people from Southeast Asia because of their darker skin color.

You might remember a young boy in the music video "Gangnam Style" called "Little Psy" because he looks and dances exactly like the Korean singer and songwriter Psy. The boy has been subjected to online racial insults because he is a child from a multiracial family. His dad is Korean and his mom is a naturalized Korean from Vietnam. Because of all the discriminatory insults, he and his family filed a complaint against "bullies for insults" rather than wording it as "racial discrimination," because Korea has no anti-discrimination law.[5] Attempts to pass such legislation have met heavy resistance.

Resistance against the Homophobic, Politically Religious Right Christ

One such proposed law was the revised anti-discrimination bill proposed by the Democratic United Party lawmakers Kim Han-gil and Choi Won-sik, but it was withdrawn in April 2013. "Facing a severe backlash and an onslaught of complaints about the anti-discrimination bill from certain conservative Christian organizations, the two lawmakers in effect raised the white flag of surrender. . . . If passed, the bill could have banned all unreasonable discrimination based on gender, disability, medical history, age, language, nationality, ethnicity, physical conditions including skin color, religion, ideology and political orientation, sexual orientation, educational background, and employment status."[6]

This was not the first time that conservative Christians blocked anti-discrimination legislation in Korea. In 2007 and 2010 conservative Christians likewise opposed the anti-discrimination bill because they believed that it would allow people to praise North Korean communist ideology and legalize homosexuality. According to the two lawmakers, conservative Christians have even labeled them as "pro-North, gay lawmakers" in an attempt to insult them into non-action. Rev. Hong Jae Chul, president of the Christian Council of Korea, when interviewed by a major media network, threatened, "The Democratic United Party should choose either a few homosexuals or the Korean Christianity of 1,200,000 members. If the Anti-Discrimination law passes, 1,200,000 Christians will protest against it before the National Assembly."[7]

Some conservative Christians have claimed that if an anti-discrimination law is passed, pastors will not be able to preach that homosexuality is a sin, and schools will not be able to punish people who teach or support homosexual activity or who praise North Korea. They have asserted that such a law would violate their freedom of religion and expression. In 2007 they even advertised anti-anti-discrimination law slogans in the newspaper. The slogans themselves were terribly insulting and discriminating toward LGBTQI people. They included statements such as "How can you imagine that your daughter-in-law could be a man? What the hell is homosexuality?" They even created a term, "Jongbook gay," which means, "Pro–North Korea commie gay," in order to use homophobia to suppress the political and religious left and maintain their power.

The controversy over anti-discrimination legislation all too clearly demonstrates the state of human rights in Korea and reveals the hidden face of mainstream Korean Christianity. This version of Christianity is too often invoked to preserve the privilege and power of political conservatives in the name of a politically Religious Right Christ—a homophobic, anti–North Korea, pro-white Christ. The politically Religious Right Christ has persuaded conservative Korean Christians to believe that it is all right for them to neglect, insult, and discriminate against people of different sexual orientation or gender identity and those with differing ideological or religious opinions, painting them as sinful, anti-Christ, and satanic. The dominant Christ encourages Korean Christians to foment and spread discrimination and hatred in the name of God. Korean Christians urgently need to resist this racist, homophobic, exclusionary portrayal of Christ in order to be in solidarity with the Christ hidden in suffering outcasts.

Concluding Thoughts

W. E. B. Du Bois described the problem of the twentieth century as a problem of "the color line." The current problem of Korea is the intersectional problem of the color-class line, the gender identity-sexuality line, and the political-ideological line. In the last six years the power structure of Korea has been constructed only for Koreans (or at least "white-ish" persons) who are heterosexual, upper-middle class, and politically right. A conservative Presbyterian megachurch elder and former South Korean president, Lee Myung-bak,[8] contributed much to building this power structure within the economic system. Furthermore, Korea's current president, Park Geun-hye, who frequently mentions that her political philosophy derives from her father, Park Chung-hee, a well-known military dictator, has worked to concentrate this power structure through the rewriting of Korean history in light of her political and ideological perspectives.

Of course, there are Christians who have dedicated themselves to work and struggle with outcasts in Korea. One McCormick Theological Seminary graduate, Rev. Kim Hae Sung, has made a big change against unconscious discriminative ways of everyday life in Korea. There used to be a light peach color of crayons and watercolor paints in Korea called "skin color." Rev. Kim used legal channels to change the name of the color to "apricot color" instead of "skin color," since the name itself discriminates against people whose color is different from that specific apricot color. This is a small example of what Christians have been doing to follow Christ hidden in the suffering of outcasts in Korea.

Yet, a growing number of Korean Christians publicly reject and discriminate against people on the margins in order to protect and proclaim their Christ with their faithful hearts. I would like to acknowledge that what they are trying to do is what they have been taught and sincerely believed in as Christians. However, as they see the issues of human rights twisted to what they identify as issues of faith, sin, and the anti-Christ movement, Korean Christians become a huge obstacle to the progressive movement for human rights and protection of human dignity. Some non-Christian Koreans call Korean Christians "pro-discrimination people" because of their lack of support for eliminating discrimination. Furthermore, non-Christian Koreans are urging Korean Christians to remember the commandment "Do to others what you would have them do to you." This dynamic reminds me of what Jesus said in Luke 19:40: "If they keep quiet, the stones will cry out." I would like to cry out to conservative Korean Christians to listen to "the stones' cry" rather than to their distorted version of Christ.

NOTES

1. Reggie L. Williams, "Dietrich Bonhoeffer, the Harlem Renaissance, and the Black Christ," in *Bonhoeffer, Christ and Culture,* ed. Keith L. Johnson and Timothy Larsen (Downers Grove, IL: InterVarsity Press, 2013), 59–72.

2. This abbreviation stands for "lesbian, gay, bisexual, transgender, queer, intersex" community (http://www.lgbt.ucla.edu/documents/LGBTTerminology.pdf).

3. Sang Bok Ha, "Yellow Skin, White Masks: A Historical Consideration of Internalized Racism in Korea and Multiculturalism," *Journal of the Institute for Humanities & Sciences 33* (June 2012): 535–36.

4. The translation is adapted from http://www.jpopasia.com/lyrics/18352/t/black-happiness.html; I revised some of English phrasing. Used by permission of the website and translator.

5. For more information, see http://www.koreabang.com/2013/stories/little-psy-subject-of-online-racial-hatred.html.

6. "The Need for Anti-Discrimination Legislation," *The Hankyoreh*, April 22, 2013 (http://english.hani.co.kr/arti/english_edition/e_editorial/583971.html).

7. For news and more information, see http://news.khan.co.kr/kh_news/art_print.html?artid=201305152224545.

8. http://en.wikipedia.org/wiki/Lee_Myung-bak.

6

Home Sweet Diaspora Home

ARAM BAE

My parents left me at church when I was ten years old. When my friends and I returned from our ritual Sunday trip to the Burger King right around the corner, my parents were nowhere to be found. Shocked and confused, I called home. In a matter-of-fact voice, my mom told me that they had left with my younger brother and were already home. My family had left me behind! My very own parents had left me behind with church folks, with adults who didn't know my favorite color or about my most recent crush—adults who were clueless about my boy band obsession, my latest fashion craze, or the most recent drama among the fifth graders in Sunday school. They left me among elders and deacons who barely knew me. These adults didn't know my hobbies, but still they showered me with gifts every Christmas, hugged me tightly every Sunday, and complimented my manners every time it mattered. These people cared about my dad, their pastor, and they cared about me too. My parents had left me with people who loved me like family. Maybe my parents knew what they were doing. After all, at family gatherings everyone has a ride home.

The Korean immigrant church is my second home. As with most homes, there is a time to be at home and a time to be away, and sometimes the farther away the better. As a child and a teenager, it was necessary and good for me to be "at home." Sunday was, in fact, my favorite day of the week. If star stickers had been given out at church as they were at school, my weekly attendance card would have been covered with them. I was a star church child who faithfully recited weekly Scripture passages, belted out Sunday school songs to her choir director's delight, and even won a medal for being a good leader among her sixth-grade peers. To top it all off, being a pastor's child, I had immediate approval from other parents. All the adults favored me, and I basked in that favor.

There were, however, aspects that I disliked, or rather did not fully appreciate until becoming an adult. For example, unlike my school peers, Saturday mornings were not about cartoons and breakfast in pajamas. Instead, Saturday mornings were Korean school days. In other words, Saturdays were get-in-touch-with-your-heritage-and-recite-the-Korean-national-anthem kind of days. My childhood Saturday mornings were filled with hours of writing Korean sentences, reading Korean folklore, reciting Korean poems, singing traditional Korean songs—all things Korean. As a child, I hated it. I vowed that I would never force my children to go to school on a weekend. Now, decades later as an adult, I know that I will put my child through the same kind of regimen, the same kind of blessed tradition. It is because of my parents' mandatory insistence of Saturday morning Korean school that I am able to worship alongside my parents' generation in my mother tongue. I can read the call to worship in Korean, sing hymns in Korean, recite the Lord's Prayer in Korean, even understand parts of the sermon in Korean.

If the Korean immigrant church fundamentally shaped my cultural identity as a Korean American during my childhood, it also significantly laid the foundations of my faith identity during adolescence. By the time I turned thirteen and was old enough to join the youth group, my attachment to the Korean church had only intensified. Friday night, with its youth group meetings, became my favorite time of the week, with Sunday being the second. I was hardly popular at school, but I sure was popular at church! I was elected to be a youth group officer not once but twice. The youth pastor—whoever that happened to be that particular year—and I worked closely together, as if I was on par with an adult. Youth group members trusted me with their problems. I had a role, an important role.

As far as I could tell, my faith journey was going splendidly. Memorizing Scripture, increasing my prayer time, and praising with my hands held high proved that I was maturing in faith, that I was becoming a good Christian girl on the right path. High school was awful, but my church life made adolescence bearable. Being one of the few Asians at my local high school in Richmond, Virginia, I felt like a minority. Church, however, was different. I was nobody at school, but I was somebody at church. My church, the Korean American faith community, was a place for me to grow, both spiritually and emotionally. The church became my escape from the "90210" horrors of high school. Church provided a survival guide through my adolescence, a wellspring for self-esteem. The Korean church, in essence, gave me an identity that I could claim proudly.

It was at church that I had the entire day to spend with friends who looked like me, had names similar to mine, and shared the same complaints about their ethnocentric parents. At church there was no need to explain my ethnic origin or even be asked if I was Chinese or Japanese. I did not have to explain the kind of after-school snacks found in our pantry or defend taking off my shoes upon entering the house. Time at church was time to be myself without having to worry about what my non-Korean peers thought of me. As a child and later as a teenager, my home church, always a Korean one, was simply that—home.

Yet, like an unexpected detour on the journey, this once-upon-a-happy-place of mine now has its way of infuriating the good church girl out of me, so much so that I want to run away from it—far, far away. I want to run away from the overt sexism and stifling nature of patriarchy found in the church. I want to run away from the ageism that works against me. I want to run away from the sometimes subtle but always telling way certain older adults have when they speak to me, or rather, speak *at* me. I want to run away from the uncritical dissemination of the Christian faith, creating indoctrinated church folk rather than fostering a faith-seeking-understanding generation of Christian thinkers. I want nothing to do with the singular, narrow agenda of conservative theology that values traditionalism over tradition. I want to distance myself from preachers who appear to love dogma over ethics, a suffocating homogenous community that makes no room for my LGBTQ friends, and a pervasive, uncritical practice of hierarchy. And I really want to stay away from adults who, having been spoiled by both their parents and culture, still expect women to remain ignorantly agreeable, alluringly quiet, and alarmingly thin. I want to run away from it all. I want to run away from this place I once loved and stay away, because sometimes it is easier to leave and find a new home than to fix the one in which you were raised.

Much More than a Church

The role of the Korean American church in the lives of second-generation Korean Americans is a multifaceted one, and, like me, many people describe it as a home away from home. In *East to America: Korean American Life Stories*, professors Elaine H. Kim and Eui-Young Yu share a collection of short autobiographical stories from Korean Americans of various backgrounds. By sharing the lives of everyday people rather than only of professionals or academics, the editors were hoping to create "not simply a call for Korean American visibility, but also a bid for Korean American participation in establishing the terms of that visibility."[1] Their efforts are commendable, and the collection is quite diverse. The content of the stories is wide-ranging, including negotiating identity crises, experiences of marginality, celebrations, generational gaps, marital woes, ethnic pride, and advice concerning men from a "very pragmatic" mother.[2]

Although the project has no religious agenda, and the stories reflect several faith traditions, both Kim and Yu recognize the significant role of the church in the lives of most Korean Americans. They observe, "Whether their American life is experienced as sanctuary or purgatory, many Korean Americans consider their ethnic community organizations essential to their immediate psychic and material survival [and] Christian churches, most of them Protestant, have become the most important community organization for Koreans in the United States."[3] Reflecting this is a running joke among Koreans that displays more ethnocentric pride than humor. It goes something like this: When the Chinese immigrate to the United States, they start restaurants; the Japanese invest in business; and the Koreans build churches.

While the average churchgoer may attribute the significant trend of church growth within the Korean American community as a sign of divine blessing for a chosen people, historians and religious scholars attribute it to the political and socioeconomic conditions in which the Korean immigrant church had its beginnings. One must first examine, however, the historical context of Korean immigration and its relationship with the Christian faith in order to appreciate fully the role of the church in the Korean American community as a home away from home, which ultimately has consequential influences for the way one thinks critically.

Jung Ha Kim, a professor at Georgia State University whose main work focuses on the interplay between gender and the sociology of religion, has done extensive research on the history of Korean churches in the United States, noting patterns of feminization, the permanence of patriarchy, and an ethos of religion (one's actions) over faith (one's beliefs). In her assessment of the first Korean churches established during the first half of the twentieth century, Kim argues, "What brought Korean Americans together to form a faith community is not necessarily their affiliation with the same religious identity, but their shared experiences of being 'Korean' in the United States during this historical time period [between 1903 and 1950]."[4] She argues, therefore, that the first wave of Korean immigration that began on January 13, 1903, logically and necessarily involved the creation of the first four Korean American churches within the first two years of immigration, but that this was for psychological and cultural reasons more than for religious ones.

In fact, in her later essays Kim takes a step further back and recognizes the underlying political conditions that led to the creation of the first Korean churches in the United States. She writes:

> Given the legal constraints barring Korean Americans from becoming U.S. citizens, Korean Americans' nationalism to actively participate in the movement for Korean independence from Japan may have been further ignited. . . . Indeed, most surviving records from this time period testify to unusually frequent gatherings at the church and active participation of "churched" Korean Americans in the Korea Independence. The importance of the Christian church providing a physical site for Korean Americans to gather together to "donate significant portions of their wages to support the provisional government" and providing a religious cause for its adherents to repeatedly sign and send numerous petitions to U.S. president Theodore Roosevelt advocating Korean national independence cannot be exaggerated.[5]

Thus, Kim underscores political reasons as the ultimate pull factor for gathering as a racial ethnic church: the greater good of the homeland. A visceral connection to the motherland was a primary reason for the initial booming church growth. In its beginning stages, therefore, the church in the Korean American community functioned for a purpose even greater than emotional or cultural survival. Newly arrived immigrants in the United States were invested in the survival of their home country. The church, therefore, was not only and understandably a home away from home, but also a place where one could participate in the preservation of one's true home.

When we consider ways in which the present Korean American church functions within the Korean American community, the image of a home away from home becomes even more evident. Kim reasons, "As a people in exile whose experiences are marked by double colonialism, Korean Americans have formed and founded their faith community in the United Sates in their own racial-ethnic churches."[6] Writing from a sociological perspective, Kim defends such ethnic solidarity as a justifiable means of survival in a new country. She argues, "Quite naturally, then, ethnic solidarity among Korean immigrants serves as a necessary social device to ensure their own ethnic community. [Sociologist S. Dale McLemore] saw that ethnic solidarity assists immigrants by performing dual functions: adjustment to the demands of the host society and reinforcement of the way of life they have left behind."[7]

Thus, for immigrants the church serves as a way to cope with this sense of loss and longing and is a means to reestablish identity. Kim comments:

> As an ethnic "minority" group in the United States, Korean-Americans experience both a sense of loss of their social identities through "desocialization" . . . and homogenization . . . in the host society and a sense of ethnic solidarity based on a commonly shared struggle to maintain their native culture and ethnic pride. Among many Korean-American institutions based on ethnic solidarity, one institution in particular seems to be quite successful in healing the pains of the desocialized people and simultaneously ensuring a sense of personal worth and group identity. That institution is the Korean-American church in the United States.[8]

Like her colleagues in Asian American studies, such as Pyong Gap Min, Elaine H. Kim, and Eui-Young Yu, Jung Ha Kim's assessment of the Korean American church reflects an understanding of the experience of immigration on a homogenous ethnic community. Furthermore, beginning with the first Korean churches in Hawaii, San Francisco, and Los Angeles, "these churches became the main community centers to address multifaceted survival needs of their adherents, and they provided programs and services such as translation and interpretation, job placement, counseling, legal aids, conflict resolution strategies, and language classes."[9]

In addition to being a place for worship, the Korean American church was and continues to be a hub for social and business networking, a place where one's heritage and culture are both explicitly and implicitly taught, and most significantly, are a psychological balm for those whose lives are marked daily by experiences of dislocation and isolation.[10] Similar to other racial ethnic communities, the church becomes the place where for one day a week, if not more, one ceases to be a minority and can feel at home with others who share the same food and language. The church in the Korean American community, therefore, fulfills a social need that includes a fundamental psychological need. In these ways, the Korean American church functions like an oasis, a consistent and life-giving source of familiarity and ease.

In her description of the Korean American church as a second home, Yu writes, "For many Koreans, especially the elderly, church is their principal place of social activity . . . [providing] many kinds of educational and social service programs for new immigrants. They make friends at church gatherings, exchange information on jobs, business, social service benefits, schooling, and form the close support network necessary to cope with the pressures of immigrant life."[11] Therefore, it is clearly evident that the Korean American church plays a significant role in an individual's life and the life of the community and consequently influences the way one views oneself and others.

Homecoming

Predictably, for me college was my time to run away from my ethnic home church. I had the chance, and I took it. No longer having to be concerned about my dad's reputation as the pastor in town or my own as the resident "PK," I rebelled like a typical college kid. Seminary was a time for me to return to my religious ways, but I still kept my distance from the Korean church. This time, however, it was a matter of expanding my horizons. I made the strategic decision to fulfill my first year-long field education internship at a non-Korean church, a predominantly white congregation. It was during my time at Westfield Presbyterian Church that everything that I was learning in the Christian education classes at seminary started to make sense (e.g., the liturgical calendar, the practice of *lectio divina*, and the program year paralleling the school year, which meant the summer months were practically void of youth group activities). Later, while in Richmond, I worked again at a white Presbyterian church, hoping to expand my experiences of Christian education, particularly with adult education. I knew that all of this was a temporary change of residence; I knew that I would be returning to my ethnic home church.

I return with a renewed sense of deep appreciation and respect for my home church. I return with a commitment to be part of the change within the community that raised me. I do not come with new, fancy program ideas or some divine inspiration revealed only to me. I come with conviction fueled by passion, frustration, and still some anger, but I come mostly with hope. I hope to be part of the faithful endeavor to create a space where faith seeking understanding is explored fully.

I want to be proud of my home—God, do I want to be proud of it! I want to be part of the effort of ridding the church of its non-Christlike attitudes and practices of sexism, ageism, and homophobia. The effort will be tireless and the work challenging. Yet I choose to return to my home sweet diaspora home, living with the tension of this place that has loved and nurtured me, so that I too can be a part of its renovations, its faithful response to be a church reformed and always reforming. It sure is good to be home—God, it's good to be home.

NOTES

1. Elaine H. Kim and Eui-Young Yu, eds., *East to America: Korean American Life Stories* (New York: New Press, 1996), xxii.
2. One of my favorite essays is entitled "Hot Pepper" by Maeun Koch'u, a pseudonym with the same meaning as the title. In her anecdote she recalls her mother's advice concerning men, specifically not to trust them and instead "to be like chagun koch'u [small hot pepper]; you're small, but when someone bites into you, you've got a big kick" (Ibid., 63).
3. Ibid., xxi.
4. Jung Ha Kim, "Cartography of Korean American Protestant Faith Communities in the United States," in *Religions in Asian America: Building Faith Communities*, ed. Pyong Gap Min and Jung Ha Kim (Walnut Creek, CA: Altamira Press, 2002), 193.
5. Ibid., 191.
6. Ibid., 192.
7. Jung Ha Kim, *Bridge-Makers and Cross-Bearers: Korean American Women and the Church*, American Academy of Religion Academy Series 92 (Atlanta: Scholars Press, 1997), 13.
8. Ibid., 14.
9. Kim, "Cartography," 192.
10. Kim identifies a culturally specific purpose of the church for immigrant communities. She remarks, "One of the most common aspects that cuts across all ethnic/racial churches is the longing for stable social identities and acceptance from the dominant society. By juxtaposing these two desires for assimilation and integration into the host society holding onto the culture they left behind, ethnic/racial churches such as Korean-American churches in the United States seek to . . . meet the particular needs of transplanted people with dual loyalty and address the pain of immigrants' 'bicultural homelessness in this American wilderness'. . . . The marginal existence of Korean-Americans in the United States determines the very character and function of their churches as 'communitas'" (Kim, *Bridge-Makers and Cross-Bearers*, 15–16).
11. Eui-Young Yu, "Korean American Community Issues and Prospects," in *Korean American Ministry: A Resource Book*, ed. Sang Hyun Lee and John V. Moore (Louisville: General Assembly Council, Presbyterian Church [U.S.A.], 1993), 178.

7

Woman in Purple—Ministry in Purple

JEAN KIM

"Woman in Purple" is not a name I gave myself. I earned this nickname from people who have seen me wearing a purple shirt every day since 1997, a shirt with the words "End Homelessness" printed on it. The color purple has become my trademark and identity because of this.

Purple is the liturgical color for the season of Lent. Purple can symbolize pain, suffering, and therefore mourning and penitence. It is also the color of royalty, and so traditionally it has been used for Advent. Purple also speaks of fasting, faith, patience, and trust. Lent is the time when Christians grieve, lament, and repent with prayer and fasting for Jesus' suffering and reflect seriously upon our lives and repent of our personal and corporate sins. By wearing my purple shirt, I outwardly grieve, lament, and repent for having so many homeless people in this affluent country, and I commit to love and serve Jesus Christ by serving the homeless and to work toward ending homelessness. For this reason, I chose purple when I developed shirts as part of the campaign of the Presbyterian Church (USA) to end homelessness for all people.

Thus, the color purple has become the color for my homeless mission. Because the color purple can also symbolize pain, suffering, and mourning of homeless people who have lost their jobs, homes, families, identity, health, pride, joy, and hopes, they deserve to be called "People in Purple."

Purple also represents my own pain, suffering, and mourning for my past hurts, wounds, and many losses. Therefore, I hold the pain of my Lord Jesus, my dear homeless friends, and my own deep pain together in my heart. We share our pain with each other. My love for Jesus is my love for the homeless, and vice versa. As Jesus participates in my suffering and pain, I too participate in his as well as with the homeless.

My Own Loss

I was born into a wealthy family in Ham Heung, North Korea, in 1935. I was raised like a princess, eating the best foods and wearing beautiful clothes. However, I also grew up empathizing with and feeling my mother's anguish as my father abused her. He always had another wife and came home sporadically and beat up my mother. Perhaps I was conceived grieving in my mother's womb, as she was grieving. When I grew up, my mother's tears, grief, and anguish were my daily food. Thus, I grew up with the absence of my father's presence, care, love, and peace in a broken home. Early on, at the age of five, I developed an asthmatic cough every winter, which has lasted up to the present.

I was born in the midst of Korea's suffering under Japanese occupation (1919–1945). I remember losing our language, names, and identity. After World War II, when a communist regime settled in North Korea, my mother, siblings, and I fled to South Korea, leaving our three homes, property, friends, relatives, and our abusive husband and father behind. We were uprooted and displaced in a strange land. Loss continued in my life during the Korean War, in which I lost my eldest brother, who had been my father figure. Twice during the war we were displaced as exiles, and all of our belongings were bombed to ashes.

Then, by immigrating to the United States in 1970, I lost my native country, culture, relatives, and friends. During the 1980 economic recession we lost our new home and business. My loss and grief continued into my midlife, when, during the years 1977 and 1989, I lost my oldest son, my mother, my second oldest brother, and my second nephew, all of whom I dearly loved. The loss of a child was the most devastating. The pain felt like a piece of bombshell stuck in my heart. I moved away from St. Louis, which to me had become a city of death, and by doing so I lost all my dear friends and support system. As I've gotten older, I have also lost my husband, my youth, and a good part of my health. So my life has been a constant stream of loss and grief.

Visions

During these many decades of loss I clung to my faith. God transformed all my wounds into new energy through several visions I received to serve the homeless.

VISION 1

During my last year of high school in Korea, in the winter of 1954, our home church started a hundred-day-long dawn prayer service. My prayers revolved around what kind of a future God might be preparing for me. One early morning, while I was praying, my heart mysteriously moved toward theological education. My family had been urging me to go to medical school or law school. Studying theology was completely contrary to their wishes for me. When they learned about my vision, they all began to grieve as if they had already lost me. Yet the church leaders loved hearing my vision and guided me to Han Shin Presbyterian Seminary in Korea. It was my first sense of a call. I was nineteen years old.

VISION 2

The night before our departure from St. Louis for Seattle, I had a dream: A tall tree with leafy branches was on fire. In a moment, it turned into ashes, and in another moment, out of the ashes flowers were blooming—from fire to ashes to blooming flowers. It was an awesome sight. The entire time we were traveling from St. Louis to Seattle, I carried a vision of having a church in the living room of our new home in Seattle. After our arrival in Seattle, my vision faded. But something compelled me to read the Bible day and night for a couple of years.

VISION 3

It was May 1980 when many young people of Kwang Ju took to the streets to protest the dictatorship of South Korean president Chun Doo Hwan. He sent troops to Kwang Ju to kill many demonstrators. My husband and I were so devastated that we organized the Korean-American Human Rights Council in Seattle in order to support the grieving people of Kwang Ju for the loss of their children. We also planned a memorial service for the victims. Although my husband and I could officiate the service as theology graduates, we invited the Seattle area Korean pastors to officiate the service. However, none of them showed up, so my husband and I led the memorial service.

I was deeply disappointed by these local Korean pastors, and a vision for ordination crept into my heart. Up until then, I had never dreamed of being ordained. I told the Rev. Jack Wilson, the pastor of my church in Maplewood, about this vision. Before I knew it, the ordination process began. I was ordained on April 12, 1987, at the age of fifty-two. My first call was at the Campus Christian Ministry at the University of Washington to develop a ministry for the international students, which I developed and served for seven years.

VISION 4

One year after my ordination, on Easter night in 1988, while I was serving the students at the University of Washington, I had a dream. It was so crystal clear and awesome that I still remember it vividly. In the dream, I was standing inside the front door of a small church. There was a huge fire, and God commanded me from the fire to plant a cross where I was standing and said, "It will grow through the roof." Since I did not know how else to respond to the dream, I added more spiritual programs at the campus ministry.

One day, I was admitted to a hospital with a blood pressure of 220 and chest pain. In the hospital bed, I mumbled to God that I didn't have time to lie in bed and asked God to explain what the message about planting a cross meant. As I dozed, the whole room turned to white and the meaning of the dream became clear. I was to do ministry with homeless women. I began to wonder what good it was to have a well-paying job with good benefits if I was about to die. So I surrendered to God responding, "Yes, yes, I will do it." I thanked God for clarifying the meaning of the awesome vision.

This vision meant that God picked me up from the ashes and revived me to full life. When I lost my child, I had pushed God away and had refused to be comforted, only demanding that God let me go, abandon me, and nullify my existence. So when this vision became clear, it was the moment I welcomed God back into my life again. I ended up exclaiming, "Now I see the light, I see the light!" It was then that I decided to develop a homeless mission project.

What Is Homelessness?

What is homelessness? First, there is a government definition of (physical) homelessness:

> The term "homeless," "homeless individual," and "homeless person" means— (1) an individual or family who lacks a fixed, regular, and adequate nighttime residence; (2) an individual or family with a primary nighttime residence that is a public or private place not designed for or ordinarily used as a regular sleeping accommodation for human

> beings, including a car, park, abandoned building, bus or train station, airport, or camping ground; (3) an individual or family living in a supervised publicly or privately operated shelter designated to provide temporary living arrangements (including hotels and motels paid for by Federal, State, or local government programs for low-income individuals or by charitable organizations, congregate shelters, and transitional housing); (4) an individual who resided in a shelter or place not meant for human habitation and who is exiting an institution where he or she temporarily resided; (5) an individual or family who—(A) will imminently lose their housing, including housing they own, rent, or live in without paying rent, are sharing with others, and rooms in hotels or motels not paid for by Federal, State, or local government programs for low-income individuals or by charitable organizations. . . . (B) has no subsequent residence identified; and (C) lacks the resources or support networks needed to obtain other permanent housing.[1]

To this primary definition of homelessness I add a second term, "emotional homelessness," because I have seen so many people who are abused, hurt, broken, and deserted by their families, friends, and society. When people are so poor economically that they lose the meaning and purpose of life, and they are drowned in a negative self-image and are consumed with hatred and rage and are living a destructive lifestyle, they can become emotionally homeless. Oftentimes physical homelessness causes emotional homelessness, and vice versa. They affect one another.

I add to these two definitions a third dimension, "social homelessness." Many homeless men and women I serve don't have any family members nearby, being estranged from spouses or grown children and vice versa. Most of them have no friends with whom they can associate or count on. No one invites them. They have no place to go. They mostly waste time because no one gives them work. They are nowhere and everywhere on the streets. They seem to be very lonely, isolated, alienated, belonging nowhere, to nobody.

Finally, I added to these three definitions a fourth dimension, "spiritual homelessness." When abused children grow up identifying God with their abusive parents, when they run away from their parents and God altogether, they can become spiritually homeless. Likewise, economic suffering can become the root cause of people's spiritual homelessness when it results in hunger, homelessness, profound hopelessness, and despair that make them feel that God punishes and deserts them. Consequently, their lifestyle and behaviors can become destructive to themselves and others. They can easily walk away from God and their own life and become spiritually homeless.

They might also believe that the church and God side with their oppressors when the church is denying their access to the house of God because they are dirty, smelly, disheveled, and at times act strangely. Therefore, the behavior of those in the church can lead the homeless, as well as themselves, to spiritual homelessness. Those who consider themselves devout Christians with regular spiritual rituals—attending church, giving offerings, praying, and fasting—can also become spiritually homeless as described in the Scriptures: "I hate, I despise your festivals, and I take no delight in your solemn assemblies. Even though you offer me your burnt offerings and grain offerings, I will not accept them; take away from me the noise of your songs; I will not listen to the melody of your harps. But let justice roll down like waters, and righteousness like an ever-flowing stream" (Amos 5:21-24, NRSV). "Learn to do good; seek justice, rescue the oppressed, defend the orphan, plead for the widow" (Isaiah 1:17, NRSV).

Although I was already involved in working with homeless people through secular jobs, it took three years for me to start the Church of Mary Magdalene, which I began on January 19, 1991. This is a worshiping community of homeless women in Seattle. This, I believe, fulfills the fourth vision that I had.

Why a Church for Homeless Women?

I have met many male and female patients brought to a psychiatric hospital ward after suicide attempts. I wondered, *If God had been in their lives, would they have tried to kill themselves?* Later, when I was assigned to three homeless women's shelters as a mental health practitioner, I met many emotionally troubled homeless women. I realized that their (and also men's) spiritual needs could not be met by good mental health treatment, counseling, and case management services alone.

In both their early and adult lives many homeless women were abused and damaged physically, emotionally, and spiritually by their parental figures, spouses, partners—abuse often perpetrated in the name of God. In their homeless life they continued to be abused, robbed, raped, and even murdered. What had resulted from such experiences was a low and negative self-image, despair, and paranoia that together led to destructive behaviors to self, others, and society. I was motivated to create a worshiping environment for homeless women—and later also for men—that was safe, accepting, caring, loving, sharing, and supportive.

The name of the church came from the biblical woman Mary Magdalene, who was caught by seven demons but freed and healed by Jesus (Luke 8:2). The name was intended to offer homeless women a hope that they too might experience healing from their seven demons (poverty, unemployment, homelessness, despair, hopelessness, mental illness, and substance abuse), and that they may arrive where Mary Magdalene arrived, by encountering Jesus.

In order to meet such grand and inclusive goals, I developed a logo and litanies, worship, songs, healing rituals, and weekly activities, the latter held every Saturday in the basement of First United Methodist Church of Seattle. All the ministry programs and activities had one goal: to free homeless women from their sufferings, abuse, and homelessness, and to lead them to a joyful dance. In an effort to achieve all these, I developed this affirmation of faith:

> We, who are homeless or suffering from multiple difficulties, believe in God, who created and blessed women, men, and children equally in God's own image.
>
> We affirm God as a loving and forgiving God, not a condemning God. Therefore, we refuse to be treated as inferior and less worthy human beings. We loudly affirm that we deserve to dream a vision, hope, and future.
>
> We re-image Jesus Christ as our forgiving and healing mother, father, sister, brother, friend, and Savior, who himself was homeless, abused, and crucified on a cross.
>
> We affirm Jesus' resurrection as a mirror of our own healing from our poverty, homelessness, brokenness, bondage, and destructive thoughts and actions.
>
> We affirm the Holy Spirit as the source of our strength and inspiration who raises us from every fall. The Spirit constantly leads us back home in God.
>
> We affirm our gathering as a worshiping community that practices love, joy, peace, forgiveness, security, and support for one another.
>
> Amen.

By reciting the affirmation of faith, homeless women have learned to replace their negative image with the positive one that was originally created and intended for them. By claiming who they are intrinsically, they have been able to restore their broken lives. Our worship program included hot meals, singing with dancing, and worship with a conversational sermon and prayers. Through our communal worship, these women experienced joy, peace, and relief from their frustrations, anger, and depressive feelings. They were building a cohesive supportive community.

A few realities drew me into serving the homeless. I usually present these realities to motivate other churches to engage in the mission of ending homelessness. The first reality is that the United States is one of the wealthiest nations in the world. According to reporting from Credit Suisse, the U.S. is home to 14.2 million of the world's 35 million millionaires.[2] Eight of the top 10 of the world's billionaires are Americans.

The United States's nuclear, military, and technological power is superior. Many of us who live in the U.S. are blessed with an education, jobs, families, places to live, pride, and dignity. Korean immigrants, including me, are blessed to put our roots down in this fertile soil. Many of us can sing songs of blessings.

The second reality is poverty in the United States. Forty five million people live in poverty, three million people experience homelessness every year, and one million are homeless on any given night. The homelessness of the elderly, veterans, and families with children is an unprecedented phenomenon. One out of every four homeless persons is a child. Forty percent of homeless people are the working poor. Poverty pushes children into violence. Jim Wallis, an advocate for the poor in Washington, DC, observes, "The most painful and dangerous sign of the crisis today is what is happening to our children. . . . [They are] our poorest citizens; our most at-risk population; the recipients of our worst values, drugs, and sicknesses, and environmental practices; . . . an object of our fears more than our hopes."[3] Many of these children are growing up in inner cities.

The third reality is poverty and racism. It is reported that forty-five million Americans suffer from poverty.[4] A child is born into poverty every thirty-three seconds. More than 15 percent of Americans live in poverty, including one in five children (22 percent), the highest rate in the industrialized world.[5] The history of discrimination is a major factor in creating the ghetto environment. Past racial discrimination is still powerfully embedded in current social, political, and physical structures and thus remains a potent cause of contemporary inner-city poverty. Deliberately or not, employers screen out black, inner-city applicants. The continuing segregation of African Americans from the rest of society is undoubtedly the primary cause of urban black poverty.[6] Letty Russell, a theology professor at Yale Divinity School for over twenty-five years, presented the image of the city as a battered woman. Like a battered woman, the city suffers through cycles of violence, isolation, fear, rejection, powerlessness, blaming, and guilt. Cities are victims of violence.

The fourth reality is the drug culture in our society. Hal Recinos, Professor of Church and Society at Perkins School of Theology, notes that "18 percent of infants in America born in city hospitals are substance addicted. . . . Drug-related crimes cause jails to fill each day with teenagers doing heavy time."[7] He sees the violence and drugs in the city as, in part, byproducts of the structures of racism and continues, "The church has failed to address the problem of drugs and urban violence associated with the international drug trade," which has taken its heaviest toll among young Latino and African American men.[8]

The fifth reality is the feminization of poverty. The United Nations reports that 70 percent of the estimated 1.3 billion people living in poverty are women. Females are the most rapidly growing group among the impoverished. Most of the estimated one hundred million homeless people around the world are women and children. While women make up half the world population and contribute 66 percent of the hours worked each day, they earn only 10 percent of the world's income and own just 1 percent of its wealth. Six hundred million women and children live in inadequate, unhealthy shelters. Every day, some five thousand people, mostly women and children, die because of poor shelter, polluted water, and lack of sanitation. Women have few avenues by which to get out of poverty. Although they represent the majority of the world's food producers and contribute significantly to economic life everywhere, women are largely excluded from economic decisions. In most societies they lack equal access to, and control over, various means of production, including land, capital, and technology.[9]

The sixth reality is the economic system and policies that have brought an ever-widening disparity between the rich and the poor and unprecedented poverty and homelessness in the United States. According to the report "Working Hard, Falling Short," "More than one in four American working families now earn wages so low that they have difficulty surviving financially."[10]

Several other realities exist that contribute to homelessness. These include the numbers of veterans, the elderly, the mentally ill, those with serious medical problems and disabilities, the unemployed, minimum-wage earners, those who are laid off, divorced women, and ex-prisoners. Other factors include domestic violence, gentrification, lack of affordable housing and health care, slashed public assistance, lack of affordable legal services, personal crises or disasters, and injury on the job.

Researchers say that all of the above are byproducts of our economic system, which is the foremost root cause of homelessness in the United States. As observed by Richard Wilkinson and Kate Pickett:

> It is a remarkable paradox that, at the pinnacle of human material and technical achievement, we find ourselves anxiety-ridden, prone to depression, worried about how others see us, unsure of our friendships, driven to consume and with little or no community life. Lacking the relaxed social contact and emotional satisfaction we all need, we seek comfort in over-eating, obsessive shopping and spending, or become prey to excessive alcohol, psychoactive medicines and illegal drugs. How is that we have created so much mental and emotional suffering despite levels of wealth and comfort unprecedented in human history?[11]

The common problems in unequal societies are related to level of trust, mental illness including drug and alcohol, life expectancy and infant mortality, obesity, children's educational performance, teenage birth, homicide, imprisonment rates, and social mobility. There is a very strong tendency for ill-health and social problems to occur less frequently in the more-equal countries.[12]

The Bible on Poverty and Homelessness

Adam and Eve's eviction from the garden of Eden is the first case of homelessness in the Bible. When Cain was thrown out of his land after murdering Abel, when Abraham left his hometown and became a sojourner, when Jacob ran from his family and slept outdoors with a rock as his pillow, when Joseph was sold to Egypt by his half-brothers, when the Hebrews suffered under Egyptian slavery and camped in the wilderness for forty years, and when the people of the Northern Kingdom were exiled to Assyria and later the Southern Kingdom to Babylon, God's people were homeless. When God brought the exiles back to their original places, this meant the end of their homelessness. It meant coming home.

According to Jim Wallis, "In the Old Testament, the subject of the poor is the second most prominent theme. Idolatry is the first, and the two are often connected."[13] In Genesis 1:27-28 we read of how God created everyone in God's own image and blessed them equally to have a home on earth. In God's eyes, all human beings are precious. The God of the exodus is known as the liberator of Israel from Egyptian bondage. However, this same liberating God punishes whenever Israel oppresses and exploits the poor (1 Kings 21:17-19). Therefore, the people of Israel go in and out of homelessness throughout the biblical narrative, depending on their relationship with God and their neighbors—whether they are able to love God and live out God's mandate and policy for the poor.

God gave them the Ten Commandments, teaching them to love God and to love neighbors. God gave them the Jubilee law and many other laws as ways to care for the poor, and God warned the Israelites not to exploit and oppress the poor. Some of these scriptural examples include tithing for the poor (Deuteronomy 14:28-29; 26:1-15); caring for the poor (Deuteronomy 15:7-8; Leviticus 19:9; 25:35-36); not exploiting the wages of the poor (Deuteronomy 24:14; Jeremiah 22:13-14); prophets indicting Israel's complacency and coveting, oppression and exploitation of the poor, aliens, widows and orphans, and announcing the death sentence for their noncompliance (Isaiah 2:7; 3:14-15; Jeremiah 5:28-29; 22:3-5; Micah 2:2; 6:9-12; Amos 2:6b-7a; 4:1-2; 7:17; 8:4-6).

This God, who commanded to us to care for the poor and who punished Israel's noncompliance, also promised blessings to those who care for the poor and homeless:

> *Happy are those who consider the poor;*
> *the LORD delivers them in the day of trouble.*
> *The LORD protects them and keeps them alive;*
> *they are called happy in the land. . . .*
> *The LORD sustains them on their sickbed;*
> *in their illness you heal all their infirmities.*
>
> —Psalm 41:1-3 (NRSV)

In the New Testament, we read that Jesus himself was born to and raised by poor parents. He worked and died homeless. While he was on earth, he welcomed, cared for, sat and dined with, and ministered to and served the sick, disabled, sinners, tax collectors, aliens, Gentiles, prostitutes, and women. All of these people society despised, alienated, and treated as unclean social outcasts and the homeless. They were victims of the socioeconomic, political, cultural, religious system. No one was allowed to associate with them in Jesus' society. But he identified with all of these poor souls, warning us that what we do to and for them is what we do to and for Jesus himself (Matthew 25:35-46). Jesus adopted the Old Testament concept of Jubilee as the main goal of his mission: to bring good news and release to all those sufferings from poverty and homelessness (Luke 4:18-19; cf. Isaiah 61:1-3).

During his seminary years, Jim Wallis, now the executive director for the Sojourner's Community in Washington, DC, and his classmates searched through the Bible and made a discovery:

> In the New Testament, one out of every sixteen verses is about the poor! In the Gospels, the number is one out of every ten verses; in Luke's Gospel one of every seven, and in the book of James one out of every five. One seminarian found an old Bible and took a pair of scissors, and cut out every single reference to the poor. . . . When the seminarian finished, that old Bible wouldn't hold together; it fell apart. It was a Bible full of holes.[14]

Wallis claims that when we don't respond to the poor, "we cut the poor out of the Bible," and the Bible won't hold itself together. I would say that, had the same thing been done with the Old Testament, we would see worse results. Different theologians summarize our contemporary life well. Ron Sider states, "Possessions are the most common idol for rich Christians today. . . . Affluence is the god of twenty-first-century North Americans, and the adman is his prophet," and he insists that we must reject "the shower of luxuries that has almost suffocated our Christian compassion."[15]

Harvard professors Ichiro Kawachi and Bruce Kennedy write, "No matter what the level of material comfort or standard of living, Americans want more. We want to shop more and spend more to acquire an ever-expanding list of necessities and 'must-have' items."[16] They quote David W. Krueger, who said that our new disease is shopping disorder, a form of addiction that includes "compulsive shopping, competitive shopping, and revenge shopping."[17] In his book *The Present Future*, Reggie McNeal diagnoses, "The North American church is suffering from severe mission amnesia. It has forgotten why it exists. . . . The church was never intended to exist for itself. It was and is the chosen instrument of God to expand his kingdom."[18] As a result, he says, "The North American church has lost its influence . . . because it has lost its identity. It has lost its identity because it has lost its mission."[19] He concludes, "Trouble is, the church is sleeping on the job."[20] Bible scholar Bruce Larson comments, "Jesus is not condemning all the rich. . . . If you have the resources to help and choose not to, you are judged. . . . What you have is not yours; it is loaned to you for a time."[21]

Suggestions

So what are we to do about homelessness? People might say that we are doing enough already. There is some truth to this. A survey reported that 95 percent of Presbyterians are doing something to help the poor. The survey of suburban congregations in six cities of the District of Columbia and Maryland and Virginia witnessed that 60 percent of faith-based providers are sponsoring feeding programs. However, the research group, Gap Analysis, did not identify feeding and clothing as top priorities. It established housing, jobs, job training, life skill programs, mental health counseling, child care, youth services, and others as a high priority. This means that faith communities should be engaged in the prevention of and solution to homelessness.

While we celebrate all that we have been doing, we must continue to move forward from where we are because the demands for services have been rising, and homeless people cannot live by bread alone. The Presbyterian campaign was urging every church to open one room to welcome the homeless, to become partners in developing permanent housing, and to join in advocating for public policies that help these causes. I heard that the federal government calls the budget to help the poor "discretionary, not mandatory." Whether or not they set up a budget for the poor is done according to their discretion. We must challenge our policy makers to include the budget for the poor among the mandatory rather than discretionary line items of their budgets. We must also urge them to spend more of our tax money to develop more comprehensive rehabilitation programs, including housing, education, job training, child care, health care, and more to bring people out of poverty and homelessness.

For my part, I have developed 106 program ideas, which include emergency interventions, prevention, and permanent solutions. Government, social service agencies, and faith communities must all work together if we want to end homelessness.[22] I dare conclude that all of us, and Korean Americans in particular, are blessed abundantly in this country. We must share our blessings with the local poor and homeless. As Christians, we must practice the teachings of Jesus, who promised eternal life to those who helped the poor and eternal judgment to those who did not (Matthew 25:35, 45, 46). God also promised to bless us more than we give (Luke 6:38).

I am the woman in purple. Who are you? Who will you be?

NOTES

1. The McKinney-Vento Homeless Assistance Act, as amended by S. 896 The Homeless Emergency Assistance and Rapid Transition to Housing (HEARTH) Act of 2009. For more information, visit the websites of the National Coalition for the Homeless (www.nationalhomeless.org) and the National Alliance to End Homelessness (www.endhomelessness.org).

2. Robert Frank, "How Many Millionaires? Depends Who's Counting," *Inside Wealth,* http://www.cnbc.com/id/102784936 (accessed June 24, 2015).

3. Jim Wallis, *The Soul of Politics: Beyond "Religious Right" and "Secular Left"* (San Diego: Harcourt Brace, 1995), 9–10.

4. National Coalition for the Homeless, letter to the public, September 2013.

5. Danna Nolan Fewell, *The Children of Israel: Reading the Bible for the Sake of Our Children* (Nashville: Abingdon Press, 2003), 20.

6. David Hilfiker, *Urban Injustice: How Ghettos Happen* (New York: Seven Stories Press, 2002), 17–19.

7. Hal Joseph Recinos, "Racism and Drugs in the City: The Church's Call to Ministry," in *Envisioning a New City: A Reader on Urban Ministry,* ed. Eleanor Scott Meyers (Louisville: Westminster John Knox Press, 1992), 98.

8. Ibid., 101.

9. Sheryl Watkins, "Overcoming the Obstacles," *World Vision Magazine* (April/May 1997), 7.

10. Tom Waldron, Brandon Roberts, and Andrew Reamer, "Working Hard, Falling Short: America's Working Families and the Pursuit of Economic Security" (October 2004), produced by the Working Poor Families Project, a national initiative supported by the Annie E. Casey, Ford, and Rockefeller Foundations.

11. Richard Wilkinson and Kate Pickett, *The Spirit Level: Why Greater Equality Makes Societies Stronger* (New York: Bloomsbury Press, 2010), 3.

12. Ibid., 19.

13. Wallis, *Soul of Politics*, 178.

14. Ibid., 178–80.

15. Ronald J. Sider, *Rich Christians in an Age of Hunger: Moving from Affluence to Generosity, Rev. Ed.* (Nashville: Thomas Nelson, 2005), 185.

16. Ichiro Kawachi and Bruce P. Kennedy, *The Health of Nations: Why Inequality Is Harmful to Your Health* (New York: New Press, 2002), 191.

17. Ibid., 78.

18. Reggie McNeal, *The Present Future: Six Tough Questions for the Church* (San Francisco: Jossey-Bass, 2009), 15–16.

19. Ibid., 18.

20. Ibid., 19.

21. Bruce Larson, *Luke*, Communicator's Commentary 3 (Waco, TX: Word Books, 1983), 236–37.

22. For more details, see Jean Kim, "People in Purple" (5 vols.), available at http://jeankimhome.com.

8

Miracle Baby

A Life of Paradox, Science, and Miracle

MICKIE CHOI

"Science is the basic body of 'knowledge' that provides the framework for understanding natural phenomena."[1] Scientists accept and believe phenomena only when there is a considerable amount of evidence to support phenomena. This is one of the leading statements that I made in the first class of an introduction to Chemistry course that I taught at a university many years ago.

According to C. S. Lewis, there are two broad views of reality. One view is that nature is all there is. A second view is that there is something in addition to nature. Lewis calls those who hold the first view "naturalists" and those who hold the second view "supernaturalists." As a chemist, I was a naturalist and one who worked hard to contribute her skills and knowledge to science and nature. I was proud of my profession and work. Science was my life, and becoming a successful scientist was my life's goal. Searching for higher knowledge was the purpose of my life. Science was my god even before I had realized it. However, the more I achieved, the more emptiness I felt in my heart. I began to realize that there should be more to life. So I began the work of seeking the real meaning of my life.

Then, one day, Jesus came into my life. He changed my worldview and my life completely. The more I knew Jesus, the more I came to love him and became eager to serve him better and better every day.

Miracle Baby

I was born in a year of great tribulation for Korea, five days after the Korean War broke out. On that day in 1950 the North Korean Army headed for Seoul, the capital city of South Korea (officially known as the Republic of Korea). Two days later, bombing destroyed the only route from Seoul to the southern section of the country via the Han River Bridge. At the time, my parents resided in the southern suburban area of Seoul, which was very close to the Han Bridge. They barely escaped from the area invaded by the North Korean Army.

Although my refugee mother was pregnant and expecting me at any moment, she headed south on foot in the mud, for it was the rainy season in Korea. I was born en route to a mountain. With difficulty, my parents found shelter with a local resident long enough to deliver an unblessed baby. There was neither food for a nursing mother nor milk for a newborn baby. According to my parents, I was too small to be recognized as a human being due to malnutrition, and they compared my tiny infant body to that of a little rat. My mother had to keep moving to a safer place and was unable to take care of herself immediately after the delivery. I was carried by my grandmother, who was excited by the birth of her first grandchild no matter how I looked. She loved me dearly and almost sacrificially throughout her life, and she became one of the most influential people in my life.

Many people around Grandma, including my parents, still regret that I was born in the middle of such a crisis. No one could have predicted the future or the safety of anyone's life. They felt the baby should never have been born under such circumstances. One day when I was barely a week old, Grandma discovered that I was barely breathing. She continued to head south, carrying me in her arms with my parents alongside us. We were pushed by the waves of the crowd. Some of them urged her to throw the tiny body away. At some point, she finally agreed and decided to put my body wrapped in a blanket under the bush where the crowds were passing by. She continued south along with the crowd. After thirty minutes, she regretted abandoning me like that and ran back to get me, going against the crowd. She didn't expect that my body would still be there, but it was. She quickly picked me up, hugged me, and held me in her bosom with tears. With all of these unexpected events, my grandmother and my parents became separated in the crowd.

It became dark. Grandma knocked on a door in the neighborhood through which she was passing, hoping to be able to spend the night. It seemed like no one was left in the whole village. After a while, an old lady finally opened the door very cautiously. When Grandma explained her circumstances, she was welcomed inside. The old lady said that her entire family had evacuated for a safe place. She decided to stay behind because she was already old and not afraid of death. She inquired of the small wrapped item in Grandma's arms, asking what it was. Grandma answered, "Oh, this is my granddaughter. She seems to be dead. May I bury her in your backyard tomorrow morning?" The old lady pondered for a moment and went to her closet to dig out a small, round Chinese herbal tablet from her medicine chest. She said that she had saved it for an emergency for her own grandchildren, and she mixed it with water in a spoon. She opened my tiny mouth wide enough to drip the mixture into my throat. After a while, my blue-colored face gradually changed to pink. I finally began to breathe and cry! These two grandmothers were so happy, they cried and hugged one another.

God had saved me in a miraculous way!

The next morning, Grandma thanked this woman wholeheartedly and left the village with mixed feelings. On one hand, she was happy because I had come back to life again. On the other hand, she had lost her son and daughter-in-law. *How am I going to raise and take care of this baby all alone in this messy war?* she wondered with fear and anxiety.

She was weary and walked along the bank of the rice farm holding me tight. She hadn't had any food to eat the whole day. Suddenly, she heard voices calling her from a distance, "Mother, Mother!" She thought she was either hallucinating or hearing the voice of ghosts. She was scared and began to run. The voice of a man and woman came closer and closer even as she ran faster and faster. Finally a hard touch and firm grab from behind stopped her. "Mother, it's us, your son and daughter-in-law!" It was another miracle!

God's Molding

The war was over. The baby became a girl with round and big eyes in the shape of almonds. Everyone loved my big round eyes and called me "the miracle baby." How I hated that nickname! I didn't believe in miracles. I thought that if I believed in miracles, it would mean that I had to believe in the existence of God.

In his book *Miracles*, C. S. Lewis argues that a miracle is not some act that breaks the law of nature. Miracles are events that come into nature from outside; they obey all natural laws.[2] He gives several important examples to show that miraculous events don't suspend the pattern of nature indefinitely but rather, immediately upon entering nature, feed into the natural pattern. The real problem for many, including myself, is not miracles as such, but the fact that if they exist outside of nature, they may have to be attributed to a power of force, to God.

My life story is an example of "miracles" that powerfully exhibit the existence and power of God.

I was the first of four children, two girls and two boys. I was always a leader, a top student, and the center of focus and attention. I received abundant love from my grandmother, parents, relatives, teachers, friends, neighbors, and everyone around me.

I was expected to enter the top high schools in the nation. To do that, my parents transferred me to one of the best elementary schools located on the other side of Seoul when I was in the sixth grade. They made arrangements for me to stay with my uncle and his family for that last year of grammar school. I was terribly homesick and had to endure enormous amount of stress to study for the entrance examination at that early age.

I made it! I remained top of my class throughout my high school years. However, the competition was so fierce that I could not enjoy high school. I began to struggle with issues such as purpose and the meaning of life. Why did I live and study so hard, and for what? I was so self-righteous that I criticized some of my closest Christian friends. It seemed to me that they attended church not to seek God, but to meet boys. I didn't think that I needed God, whom I was not able see and touch. I was not sure of God's existence. I believed that I could handle my life on my own by working hard. These were my introvert years.

The senior year of high school is the most difficult time for students in Korea. We could enter the best college only by passing the entrance exam. Based on my academic achievement, I was supposed to apply to the top nationally ranked public school, Seoul National University. On the other hand, my father suggested that I apply either to Yonsei University (also known as the "Harvard" of Korea) or the best women's college of Korea, Ewha Women's University. Early Christian missionaries from the United States founded these two private schools in the 1800s. My father, although he was not Christian, insisted that I needed to get holistic education focused on freedom, virtues, and integrity. I disagreed with my father and insisted on going to Seoul National University only because of the academic standing. I wanted to show off who I was in terms of my GPA and academic achievements.

A few months before the college entrance exam, my left eye began to hurt. There was no apparent reason, but it produced a bloody discharge. Even after I went to see an ophthalmologist, it became worse and worse. The prescribed treatment didn't help me at all. I could do nothing but lie in bed and wait until the symptoms subsided. I took months of sick leave. When I returned to school, I found that all the preliminary placement examinations were over, and it was impossible for me to make up for lost time. I had put off until the last minute studying the subject of Korean history required by the university to which I was applying because it required mostly memorization. I discovered that I did not have enough time to take this course, and therefore I decided to apply instead to Yonsei University. That school waived the history requirement. I passed the entrance exam with ease and with excellent grades and became a college student majoring in chemistry, one field of natural science. I began to dream of becoming the next Madame Curie.

The university atmosphere was pleasant and welcoming. The only exception was the requirement of weekly chapel and mandatory Bible and theology classes for every student. Since I was neither a Christian nor one who was interested in religious subjects, I studied only to get good grades. I mainly memorized the materials at the last minute without understanding the meaning of the content, and I regurgitated knowledge on the answer sheets. Surprisingly, I always got the best scores out of hundreds of students in my freshman class. I recall those days and call them days of divine intervention and guidance.

Love and Marriage

I met my husband, Stanley Soobong Hoe, when I was a junior at Yonsei University. He joined my chemistry class after being discharged from the Korean Army. He had completed his four-year service term and was five years older than I. We were assigned to sit next to each other in our organic chemistry laboratory class. We were also in the same physical chemistry laboratory team because of the Korean alphabetical order of our last names. He would approach me subtly to assist me whenever I needed help reaching tall things (I am only five feet tall) or lifting heavy items. His gentle and caring personality made me feel comfortable around him. We would study together after school in the library as friends and competitors simultaneously.

Toward the end of my undergraduate years, we were busy and preoccupied with planning the future after graduation. One day in April, we had just returned from the last senior field trip just before graduation. Stan asked me out and abruptly proposed to me. I had had no clue that he was interested in me. He told me that he had a crush on me and had decided to marry to me from the very moment he saw me in our first chemistry class together. Apparently, he had been planning very thoughtfully and carefully about the process of approaching and proposing to me up to that moment. He also understood that I was not quite prepared for this, yet he told me to trust him. He was prepared to be patient until I was ready for the commitment, and he actually did wait.

My mother was not initially thrilled about her future son-in-law because of his family background and his upbringing by a single mother. (He was the eldest son among three children.) She, like most typically proud Korean mothers, preferred her daughter to marry a man who came from a respected family with a good, reputable name. However, she finally accepted him for his other good qualities, such as his honesty, diligence, and studiousness, along with his love and passion for me. All the professors and friends around us respected and approved of him, and they strongly recommended him to my parents as my future husband.

We married right after graduation in the winter of 1973. This was just six months before we left for the United States of America for further study together.

My Wilderness Experience and Encountering God

The moment we landed at Los Angeles International Airport, "the wilderness" desert was before us. Everything was strange and new. What a culture shock we experienced! Although we had been learning English as a second language since we were in junior high school, English was overwhelming. Neither of us was able to understand or speak the language.

We lived as poor and struggling graduate students on the campus of the University of Southern California in Los Angeles. The government in South Korea at the time only allowed those of us with a student visa to take $100 per person out of the country. We needed to live on the total of $200 that we had brought from home. Fortunately, both of us received teaching and research assistantships from school, and thus began our first semester of graduate school.

When we entered the second semester, I found out that I was pregnant. It was neither planned nor expected. Since we were not prepared financially, along with other circumstances, we were deeply troubled. In order to keep the foreign student visa status, I had to take a minimum number of classes as a full-time student. We decided that we could not keep the child. The night before the scheduled abortion, I was awake and crying in my husband's arms. I decided to become a mother.

I reorganized my research schedule according to the delivery timetable with the approval of the graduate committee. Instead of doing laboratory work immediately, which required me to handle hazardous chemicals that might harm the baby, I was allowed to do library research until the baby was delivered. My research adviser and the five graduate committee members all agreed to it. However, my adviser began to break the agreement and forced me to do some laboratory work. Coming from a cultural tradition that required absolute obedience to superiors, I didn't dare to say no. I often skipped meals because of the lab setups and ongoing experiments, and I was extremely stressed out with the pressure of the work on top of being disappointed that my adviser broke promises and took advantage of me. As an assistant professor, he had tremendous pressure to produce research results and publish articles to achieve tenure at the university. In order to do that, he had to use his graduate students as much as he could.

I became bigger and bigger with pregnancy, and I was able to feel the baby moving and kicking. It was so wonderful and awesome to have a new life inside of me. I was anxiously awaiting becoming a mother.

Sadly, but not surprisingly, I miscarried when I was almost in my sixth month of pregnancy. I actually had to go through full labor. But my doctor was not able to save my baby boy. It was the first and greatest loss that I had experienced in my life. Discharged from the hospital, I said goodbye to my adviser. Stan decided to change his major from chemistry to pharmacy. Neither of us wanted stay around that organic chemistry lab and my cruel and insensitive professor. It took us a long time to heal and recover from the emotional injuries and scars of that time.

The following year, Stan transferred to the School of Pharmacy at the University of the Pacific located in Stockton, California. I remained in Los Angeles with the intention of finishing my PhD in chemistry, but after a full year of Stan's commuting each week up and down from southern California to central California, we were exhausted. I decided to complete my master's degree at USC and then joined him for my PhD in pharmaceutical chemistry in 1978. By the time I finished with my coursework and comprehensive exams, Stan had graduated from the School of Pharmacy and secured a job back in Los Angeles. It was my turn to commute back and forth.

In the early 1980s I finally joined Stan, who was working as a pharmacist in Koreatown, Los Angeles. We settled down in Phillips Ranch, Pomona, and bought our first dream house. Finishing up my doctoral dissertation, I taught in a small school, the University of La Verne, and became pregnant once more. This time we had planned and were ready after a long period of waiting and anticipation. A healthy and beautiful girl, Danielle, was born. How happy we were!

Life seemed to be going in the right direction. Strangely enough, the more advanced scientific knowledge I acquired, the more I felt emptiness in my heart. The higher the degrees I received, the more contradictions and questions came to my mind. And my spirit was wandering. The science that was my god did not give me the full truth and answers for my existence and being. It was not "the truth" as I believed. I felt deeply troubled. My life was at stake! I began to search for the purpose and meaning of my life of as "the deer pants for the streams of water" (Psalm 42:1, NIV).

Around that time, Stan and I received news from home that Stan's younger brother, Soo Suk, had been diagnosed with early onset diabetes. He was in his early thirties. Thanks to his pharmaceutical background, Stan sent some helpful information and resources to his brother, who was a dentist. However, Soo Suk continued to neglect his health and abused himself with drinking and smoking for several years. One day, we got a phone call from Stan's sister at home that his brother was seriously ill and being hospitalized. Since Stan was not able to get time off from work, I decided to go back to Korea alone to visit him. It was a difficult reason to return for the first time since we had left so many years earlier. How much we had missed home and all the loved ones we'd left behind! How many times we had dreamed and with tears glanced westward toward the Pacific Ocean through our school dorm-room windows, wishing we could fly home like birds and see our loved ones! Now, instead of with joy and happiness, I flew the long hours home with concerns and anxiety. From the airport I went directly to the hospital where Soo Suk was. Seeing my own parents and siblings would have to wait.

All of Stan's family members and attending physicians were anxiously awaiting my arrival, since they had to make an important decision. The primary care doctor had told me that they needed to discharge him from the hospital. His condition was not getting better, and there was nothing more they could do for him. I soon found out that his uncontrolled diabetic condition had almost destroyed his body, and he was in severe pain. The doctors who had treated him previously, before he was moved into the hospital, had given him strong, morphine-type painkillers. He had become dependent and almost an addict. As it happened, he would have been a perfect case study for my PhD dissertation topic on narcotic analgesics.

I had a series of meetings with doctors and family members to discuss how to help him. The biggest problem was the patient himself. He was not listening to anyone, including the doctors, and he was asking for more painkillers whenever the effects of the drug wore off. Sometimes he became violent, especially to the nurses when the doctors were not around. I felt helpless and hopeless. My own sophisticated scientific knowledge and the modern medical technology were useless under the circumstances.

One day, Soo Suk again became restless and violent with pain, yelling for more drug injections. The doctors and nurses didn't respond. I was alone next to his bedside and didn't know what to do. All of sudden, I remembered the hymns I used to sing in the choir during my college days. Of course, I had never been a professed Christian, and I had sung the hymns without them holding any meaning for me. But there

I was, in that moment, singing those same hymns. I found myself preaching to him, "Trust and believe in Jesus Christ, whom the Bible claims as 'the Way, Truth and the Life.' He is the only God who can help you and heal you from your pain and your problems." I began to sing hymns to him one by one, and he fell asleep like a baby without any fuss and complaint.

I remembered the Old Testament passage in the book of 1 Samuel 10:13-16, regarding the spirit of God's manifestation in Saul. I realized that the spirit of God was using me, and my mouth was preaching the good news even though I had never confessed Jesus as my Lord and Savior. I was witnessing a "miracle" in front of my own eyes, one that was happening to me and my brother-in-law. Who says that there are no miracles these days? He got better and was discharged from the hospital soon after. He worked as a dentist for the next thirty years.

After that month of intensive crisis intervention with my brother-in-law and the awesome personal experience of encountering a "miracle," I returned to the United States exhausted. I did not know where or how to start sharing the whole experience with my husband. I would tell him a little bit of the story every evening when he came back home from work. However, before I could finish, I became sick with a high fever and an upper respiratory infection.

One morning, I finally awoke with the fever down and a clear mind, and I found that a whole week had passed by, and it was Easter Sunday. I called Stan and shouted at him, "Honey, hurry! We need to go to church!" He was puzzled and asked, "What? What are you talking about? Which church? We don't have a church to go to!" I yelled back him, "I don't know . . . wherever! We need to go worship the risen Lord!" We randomly attended an Easter Sunday service and later joined the Presbyterian congregation of one of our friends. We were baptized and became Christians.

God's Calling into Ministry

After Danielle was born, we worked hard to achieve our piece of the American Dream and strived to climb a ladder of worldly fame and respect. Although I had experienced miracles and professed God, I was not still quite convinced that God intervenes in the things and events of the natural world. I thought that God left the natural world to us to make better.

One night, I was trying to put my baby to sleep and was lying in bed next to her. The room was dark. I intentionally turned off all the lights. I dozed, off and on. I was not totally asleep, nor was I dreaming. Suddenly, the room seemed to be lit up, and the Lord came as a vision. He handed me a black leather-covered Bible and said, "Preach the gospel." I responded with fear: "Please give me three more months until I finish my work, Lord." Some hours passed by, and I found myself kneeling down next to the bed, perspiring and praying furiously. My body was all wet with sweat and tears. It was already morning. I ran to church for a special early morning prayer meeting that was occurring that week.

After the three months that I'd designated were up, I, of course, disregarded the experience, pretending that nothing had happened. Then, another major crisis came into my life. I had burned my right eye, this time in my laboratory. An extremely hazardous chemical, sodium hydride, which is highly explosive and flammable in the air, flew into my eye and burned it with sharp pain. I was certain that I would lose my sight. Doctors agreed with me without a doubt. However, the very next day another miracle occurred. The Holy Spirit, in the form of light who visited in my room earlier came back, touched my eye and it healed instantaneously!

This time I was unable either to deny or delay a call from God. After I had my second child, Michael, I went back to school again, this time to seminary to pursue a Master of Divinity degree. Stan was working as a pharmacist in Koreatown and helping in every way to support my education by taking care of our two children. He was such a faithful husband and wonderful father. We were so happily anticipating serving the Lord together, especially helping Korean American immigrant families that are torn apart and suffer so much between the two different languages and cultures. I believe that our prayers were precious and beautiful before God's eyes.

Then, one November day, with only two quarters left until my seminary graduation, Stan left home for work and never returned. He was robbed and killed by an unknown person in a gas station restroom in the city of Torrance while he was serving one of his patients by hand-delivering his medication. On his way home he had to fill up the gas tank before getting on the freeway. Someone was waiting for him in the restroom and attacked him. He managed to come out and collapsed next to his car. He was transported by ambulance to the nearby hospital, his skull smashed, his brain severely damaged. He was essentially dead. He was on life support for six days, but he never regained consciousness. His body was released from the coroner's office after one week. His funeral was on November 22. Two days after the funeral, it was Thanksgiving Day. Two weeks later, Stan's birthday! Two weeks after that, it was Christmas. Then it was New Year's Day. And then January 6, our wedding anniversary!

I didn't know what else to do but visit his grave on our anniversary day. While I was driving to the park, I remembered every scene of my wedding day, seventeen years earlier. It had been a cold January, a month in which few couples get married in Korea. My parents had insisted on having a wedding ceremony because we were about to leave the country for graduate school. It was rare to have flowers at that cold time of year. Fortunately, one of my mom's friends owned a flower shop and volunteered to do all the flower arrangements for the wedding. We had beautiful ivory roses!

I was hoping and praying that I could find the same roses in a flower shop at the memorial park. As soon as I opened the shop door, I saw a bucket lying in the center of the refrigerator full of the very same-colored roses! I asked the clerk for seventeen roses, and she asked me, "Are you sure? They are rather expensive." I silently calculated the number in my head and soon regretted asking for that many. Counting the roses, the clerk said to me, "Sorry, we have only a dozen left." I was somewhat relieved because I could save some money. But at the same time I also felt guilty because I thought that I was being stingy toward my dead husband.

I asked the clerk to put together a vase with the dozen roses, and I drove up to the hill and put it on my husband's grave. I could not recall a time when I had given him flowers while he was alive and with me. He was the one who would always bring me flowers, not only for special occasions but also when I felt gloomy and sad. I would often find a bunch of roses on my table in my kitchen and sometimes on my desk in my office. I had never given him any.

It reminded me of Herbert Lockyer's words in his book *All the Women of the Bible*, referring to a woman, Joanna, in Luke 8:3: "Too many save their flowers for the grave. Joanna gave hers to Jesus when He was alive and could appreciate them, as well as produce them at the tomb in honor of Him. Her 'last respects' were the outward token of the inner reverence in which she had ever held the Saviour."[3] I was the very foolish one who saved her flowers for her husband's grave! My tears were rolling down my cheeks. I learned a great lesson: People need our flowers today. Do not save them for the grave.

Ministries of Miracles

Eleven months after Stan's death I was called as a sole pastor by Zion Korean Presbyterian Church, a member of the Hanmi Presbytery. As a result, in 1992, I became the first female clergy ordained by the Korean Language Presbytery of PC(USA). That was again a miracle of God! At the time, it was virtually impossible for a woman to be called as a pastor in the Korean church context. It was even more difficult for women to pursue ordination in Korean-language presbyteries. I later learned that the Committee on Ministry and the Committee on the Preparation of Ministry of the Presbytery underwent conflict and schism on the issue of my ordination as a woman. However, God intervened and decided to place me in the place where the Lord had planned and called. People called it a "miracle."

From then on, the Lord moved me to experiencing more "miracles" in my ministry. I served as the first and only female executive presbyter of the male-dominated Korean Language Presbytery, as moderator of the Synod of Southern California and Hawaii, and as moderator of the Asian Presbyterian Council. In Korean churches, however, I was always a subject of conflict because of my gender and the untraditional style and personality of my ministry. Some Anglo colleagues referred to me as a "lightning rod."

In the early days of my ministry the voice of God came to me in Jeremiah 1:4-10:

> Now the word of the LORD came to me saying, "Before I formed you in the womb I knew you, and before you were born I consecrated you; I appointed you a prophet to the nations." Then I said, "Ah, Lord GOD! Truly I do not know how to speak, for I am only a boy." But the LORD said to me, "Do not say, 'I am only a boy'; for you shall go to all to whom I send you, and you shall speak whatever I command you. Do not be afraid of them, for I am with you to deliver you, says the LORD."
>
> Then the LORD put out his hand and touched my mouth; and the LORD said to me, "Now I have put my words in your mouth. See, today I appoint you over nations and over kingdoms, to pluck up and to pull down, to destroy and to overthrow, to build and to plant." (NRSV)

I was moved to tears when I encountered this passage from Jeremiah. God's divine will was planned way before I was aware and in a very personal way.

As a petite Korean American woman with many unique perspectives, I could relate to the prophet Jeremiah, who has been known as the Lonely Prophet, the Prophet of Tears, and the Prophet of Lament. I was called by God to speak bold prophetic messages to Korean churches as well as to the larger church in the PC(USA).

Like Jeremiah's response to God's call, our human response to God's will is often fearful and faithless. I also was fearful and afraid in every situation into which I was placed and called. For those of us who are called to preach and teach the word of God, it is always, without exception, frightening, just before we climb up into the pulpit, no matter how often we do it. For many years I pastored local congregations, and I also traveled to preach and speak throughout the United States and sometimes overseas. I have spoken to small congregations and sometimes to huge crowds. I once had a privilege to preach at the 212th General Assembly in 2002, held in Columbus, Ohio. When the moderator invited me to preach at the closing worship service, I was overwhelmed. Like Jeremiah, I responded by saying, "Why me, God? I don't know how to do it!"

When I reflected carefully upon this passage and my own attitude, I discovered why I am fearful and afraid. It is because of a lack of faith. Instead of depending upon God, I depend on my own knowledge and my own ability. I want to be in control. Western culture seems to emphasize that the person who earns respect is the one who controls every circumstance, who is self-confident and self-sufficient. I don't like not being in control. I have to perform with excellence in every situation and show and prove to people that I am somebody, and I can do it, and I am in control. That is why I was fearful and scared—because I depended on myself, not on God and the Holy Spirit, and because I was faithless. However, I believe that God has a prescription for us.

The sufficient power to overcome our fear and faithlessness comes from God. In Jeremiah 1:8 God says, "Do not be afraid of them, for I am with you to deliver you." God can and will remove our fears. In the Bible, from beginning to end, God's message is always same: "Be not afraid." To Abraham, Moses, and Jeremiah, God says, "I will be with you," and later to Mary and to Jesus' disciples, "I will be with you always, until the end of the world." Again, Jeremiah 1:9 explains, "Then the LORD put out his hand and touched my mouth; and the LORD said to me, 'Now I have put my words in your mouth.'" God had already prepared a message for Jeremiah to preach. When God calls us, God prepares everything for us. The Spirit equips us for service.

Yet ever since I was called as the first female ordained minister of word and sacrament and pastor of a struggling Korean American congregation in southern California, whose culture was male-dominated and repressive of women, I had been complaining to God, saying, "Lord, it's not fair. Why me? I cannot do it anymore." However, the Lord continued to do God's work through me.

After fifteen years of serving Korean churches, I was totally burned out. I cried out to God, "You must have reasons why you have extensively trained me from the local congregation to the Presbytery, to the Synod, and to some General Assembly responsibilities, covering the entire four governing bodies of the PC(USA). I am tired of serving Korean churches. Can you move me to a larger context of ministry? I could still help Korean churches if you want me to."

And then, the PC(USA) Investment and Loan Program, one of the six General Assembly agencies, came to me and offered me my current position as a Development Specialist/Regional Representative of the West Coast office. Although I had many graduate degrees, I had neither a financial nor a marketing background. In addition, the position required both the federal government's Securities and Exchange Commission and the New York Stock Exchange and National Association of Securities Dealers stockbroker exams. Investment bankers are the ones who study and pass those exams to get the licenses.

It was impossible for me to pass those exams, given my lack of knowledge in the area. But with another "miracle" of God, after a couple of months of study, I passed the exams and obtained the license that I needed. I have been serving the larger church for almost a decade now.

No matter how fearful and scared I was, God always removed my fears and equipped me to do the ministry. The Lord is continuously doing the same in my life and ministry. God has always been faithful, fulfilling the promise to allow me to provide for and raise my two children, Danielle, now thirty-three years old, and Michael, twenty-eight, as Father of the fatherless. Both of them graduated from Ivy League universities and graduate schools. The biggest joy that I have at the present time is being a grandmother. Michael and his wife, Chrystal, have a beautiful daughter, Eliana, who is now two years old.

Donald MacKay says in his book *Science and the Quest for Meaning*, "A God who is trustworthy is the guarantee to the scientist that natural events will not break precedents unless God has a special reason to do so; the scientist can thus rely from day to day on this expectation, based on the systemic observation of precedent which we call science."[4] I agree with him, but I also have seen on many occasions in my life that God had special reasons to break precedents.

God is real and does wonders! God performs miracles!

NOTES

1. Eleanor Dantzler Siebert, *Foundations of Chemistry* (New York: McGraw-Hill, 1982), 1.
2. C. S. Lewis, *Miracles*, new ed. (New York: HarperCollins E-Books, 2009), 42.
3. Herbert Lockyer, *All the Women of the Bible: The Life and Times of All the Women in the Bible* (Grand Rapids: Zondervan, 1988), 78.
4. Donald M. MacKay, *Science and the Quest for Meaning* (Grand Rapids: Eerdmans, 1982), 48.

PART III

Korean American Sermons

9

Standing Tall

IRENE PAK

> Now [Jesus] was teaching in one of the synagogues on the sabbath. And just then there appeared a woman with a spirit that had crippled her for eighteen years. She was bent over and was quite unable to stand up straight. When Jesus saw her, he called her over and said, "Woman, you are set free from your ailment." When he laid his hands on her, immediately she stood up straight and began praising God. But the leader of the synagogue, indignant because Jesus had cured on the Sabbath, kept saying to the crowd, "There are six days on which work ought to be done; come on those days and be cured, and not on the Sabbath day." But the Lord answered him and said, "You hypocrites! Does not each of you on the Sabbath untie his ox or his donkey from the manger, and lead it away to give it water? And ought not this woman, a daughter of Abraham whom Satan bound for eighteen long years, be set free from this bondage on the Sabbath day?" When he said this, all his opponents were put to shame; and the entire crowd was rejoicing at all the wonderful things that he was doing. (Luke 13:10-17, NRSV)

"Wow, you're tall," I've often been told. I have always been tall—for an Asian American woman. I guess it's because my parents are pretty tall for Korean folk. In elementary school I was unfortunately "blessed" with a growth spurt before everyone in my class. In my sixth grade class picture you can find me dead center on the back row, a full head taller than the tallest boy, Andrew. He so hated that I was much taller than him that he is posing sideways with his chest out. I remember noticing he was standing on his tippy toes.

As the only person of color in that classroom (and in the entire school besides my younger sister and brother), my unusual height only produced more ridicule than I was already receiving. Oh, and I was also a Presbyterian Christian among a sea of Mormons. I was nicknamed the "Jolly Green Giant" and the "Empire State Building," and was ridiculed for being different. I learned at a young age literally and figuratively to "bend over" or "bend down" so that I could attempt to blend in. I tried to make myself as "white American" as possible in speech, attitude, clothing—anything. And as I got older, I refused to wear heels or any style that would accentuate my height yet more. I grew up feeling ashamed of being Korean, of being tall, of being different. I so devalued my own identity and sense of self that I distinctly remember believing that if only I were white, blond-haired, and blue-eyed, then boys would like me, and if I were Mormon, I would have so many more friends.

Imagine then my own sense of shock and fear when, as a teenager, I first felt that call of God on my life to go into ministry. You should have heard my prayer: "Uh, God? I'm not sure if you've got the right person. Pastors are old, they're mostly white, they're men, and they're super holy. I am not any of those things. I think you have the wrong person." And I bent back down into trying to blend in.

Over the years, God drew me into following that call despite my bent state. In fact, it was an older white man who empowered me and gave me opportunities to preach, teach, and lead. For his sensitivity to my bent state and my gifts, I will always be thankful. But it was such a battle for a long time. Despite feeling empowered in one church setting, in other Christian settings, such as my college campus ministry, I was still surrounded by voices telling me that women "shouldn't lead" men. They would quote Scriptures to back this up. Yet instead of shrugging off my call, I really wanted to be attentive and honest about what it was God might be calling me to do. In retrospect, I also wonder if I wanted a way out. God continued to call. But it wasn't until I was into my twenties that God helped me recognize that I had freedom to stand tall—to embrace myself wholly and fully as God had created me to be and to declare that identity with pride.

In today's Scripture lesson, we have the story of Jesus' encounter with a woman who had a self-image and spirit that had crippled her for more than eighteen years. She was bent over and quite unable to stand up straight. Maybe her self-esteem was so damaged by eighteen years of being put down, misunderstood, and ridiculed that she felt she didn't deserve to stand tall. She definitely didn't feel as if she could ask Jesus to heal her. He had to be the one who made the first move. And thank goodness he did.

When Jesus saw her, when he noticed her, when he paid attention to her in the middle of his busy life and schedule—in the middle of a sermon—he called her over and said, "Woman, you are set free, you are set free, you are set free from your ailment." And then he touched her life, he touched her heart, he looked into her eyes and helped her to start looking up and not at the ground. He lifted her gaze toward him, toward God, and released her from her fear, from those things that were pulling her down, from the pressures of conforming to the world; and he helped her look up, to stand tall, to be proud, to live into the wholeness and the fullness of who God created her to be.

Slowly but surely, she stood up straight. She was healed. She was changed, and she was transformed from the inside out. She had become a new person, but more importantly, she had become the person whom God created her to be in the first place. Then and only then—when she was healed and free from the things that were pulling her down—could she really begin praising God with all, and not just part, of who she was.

This isn't just my story, and it isn't just the story of the woman in Luke's Gospel. In some ways, this is part of a broader story. There are things that pull us down, that bind us, and Christ brings an amazing freedom and unbinding that can unleash amazing praise. I have witnessed that and have participated in it. It is good news for all of us!

What strikes me in this story is that this healing and unbending also produce a strange fear among some of the people. I can hear the negative whispers and worry. "She's *supposed* to be bent over—what is she doing? There are other days, other times, other venues for healing. Why would Jesus do this today?" A person who finds full freedom in Christ, as this woman in the story did, is transformed and changed, and this shift can freak people out. A person might change in ways that we're not comfortable with, and might change things that we were quite comfortable with and do not appreciate being changed!

The leader of the synagogue can't see the overarching miracle that has happened because he's focused on the technicalities of when and how. He's not saying that she cannot be healed; he's just saying that today's not the time for it. The leader is not saying that she is not welcome, but simply that for now we should keep her the way she is. We're not ready for her to stand up and praise in that way.

Too often, this message is the underlying message that I hear within the context of the church.

I served my first church and my first call for four years. It was a Korean American church, and I served as the English Ministry and Christian Education associate pastor. I was the associate pastor who preached every week. I was the first woman to be called there as a pastor, and for the entire four years I was there I was the only woman on Session. It was a huge blessing in many ways, and a huge burden in many other ways. Even the youth, all of whom I loved and who sustained my energy for ministry, struggled to call me "pastor." The title "pastor" was so strongly associated with men that many of the youth started calling me "pastoress" to feminize the word. Eventually it became a term of endearment for some of them, but nonetheless I did some education about why it was important that they call me "Pastor Irene."

The burden of serving there was the back and forth I felt between identities that I understand and yet do not understand. The rift in understanding had to do with cultural differences between "Korean" and "American" assumptions. It was a strange juxtaposition when I heard, on the one hand, "Be with us, you are a part of us and our community of worship," and on the other hand, "You are supposed to stay bent over for now; it is not time yet for your healing."

Within the context of the Korean American church, I wonder when we will come to a point where we stop confusing Confucianism with Christianity. For now, we respect the role of pastor, but we are not sure what to do when that pastor is a woman or younger or single.

The fact that I culturally understand the phrase "I'm sorry, but women must be considered last," used when it comes to nominating elders within some Korean churches, does not make it okay. Actually, the fact that I "understand" it is what bothers me the most. That I as the pastor have to fight over and over for our faithful youth to be allowed to become full members of the church with the full right to vote in congregational meetings (let alone be considered for nomination to any leadership role) frustrates me to no end. How long do we remain silent? How long do we remain patient? How long do we remain bent? How long is it okay to keep others bent and silent?

There is disconnect between welcoming people into the church and making sure that many of them are still bent. It is shocking. I hear older church members ask, "Where are the second and third generations going? Why can't we get them to come to church? Why can't we get them to come back to the Korean church after they go off to college?" The answer is becoming more and more clear to me: young people do not see these churches as *their* church. They have no ownership of the church, they are seldom empowered by the church, and we in the church seldom make room for young people and for women to express the freedom that they have found in Christ. Even as I loved the ministry during that time, I am convinced that I would not have been nurtured as a young leader or woman had I felt the original call of God on my life in that context.

Because we live in a culture and world where women are still unequal—where as an Asian American woman I am sexualized into a submissive caricature, where even as a pastor myself I still don't think of an Asian woman when I hear the word "pastor"—finding the courage to stand up at General Assembly,[1] along with two other Korean American clergywomen, and speak against a committee recommendation to form another same-language (Korean) presbytery was something that I had to psyche myself into doing. I accepted this calling to ministry knowing that it would be difficult, yet struggling with the fact that I am still a voice crying out in the wilderness. I wanted to be Sarah and not Hagar. But to our surprise, the recommendation failed to pass a vote of the General Assembly. To be heard on that General Assembly floor and see the vote swing as it did like that on that day shocked me. I couldn't believe that my voice made a difference. I couldn't really feel the joy that others were proclaiming because I was suddenly deeply afraid and I wanted to bend down again, hoping to go unnoticed. Even as I can testify boldly to the freedom that I have in Christ, there are times I still struggle to stand tall because I too am afraid of the fearful whispers and shame that I may bring to myself, the church I serve, and to my family.

But I know I need to stand. I need to stand not only for myself, but also for the cloud of witnesses who have gone before me, who have paved the road and broken through the low ceiling so that I could stand tall. I need to stand for the young Korean American girl who doesn't know where her call to ministry is coming from and doesn't know any women in a pastoral role but still senses that call. I need to stand tall for the roots of my faith and my theological perspective for the one who thirsts for God but fears that there is only one way to drink deeply from the well—a way that he or she thinks is inaccessible. But most of all, I need to stand tall because Jesus saw me when I was bent. He came and laid his hands upon me, and through his life he gave me freedom. If I truly believe that I am free in Christ, then I need to stand tall in that freedom and give praise to God. I need to stand tall even when that freedom scares me, and others, because we can no longer control what I do living in the freedom that comes from God.

It is still difficult at times, but nowadays I do stand tall (sometimes I even wear heels!), and I am proud of all that God has created me to be, as a Korean American, as a Christian, as a woman, as a pastor, and as a daughter of God.

My prayer is that all of God's created beings will find the freedom to stand tall and live into who and what they are created to be. I pray that all of us will be able to be the presence of Christ for those who are currently bent over, to untie and unloose the bonds that hold people down. And I pray that if we are the ones who are keeping people bent down by placing our traditions and laws above the healing of people, we will dare to repent. Because ultimately, what really matters isn't the rules, cultures, or what we're comfortable with, but rather that all that we are and all that we do is in praise of God our Creator. Standing tall, my prayer is that we can praise God with the fullness of who we are and bring others rejoicing with us.

NOTE

1. General Assembly is a meeting of the Presbyterian Church (USA) composed of elected representatives from regional groups that meet every two years.

10

What to Expect When You're Expecting

Reflections on the Season of Advent

JOANN HAEJONG LEE

> In those days Mary set out and went with haste to a Judean town in the hill country, where she entered the house of Zechariah and greeted Elizabeth. When Elizabeth heard Mary's greeting, the child leaped in her womb. (Luke 2:39-41, NRSV)

Growing up, life never took on a reliable rhythm I could trust. While some families have holiday and birthday traditions or cycles of the year that signal times for vacation or new adventures, our family never quite fell into that kind of regularity.

My parents were first-generation Korean immigrants who owned a small business. Some immigrants are amazing entrepreneurs whose businesses are wildly successful or can at least provide a good, steady income. My parents and their business were not this way. For us, owning a small business meant that we never knew how much money we would have at the end of the month, and most of the time we would find it was not enough to pay all the bills that were due.

This kind of month-to-month uncertainty made us operate in survival mode, and we never could settle into life in the United States enough to develop traditions for Christmas or

Easter, birthdays or summertime. Sometimes there were presents; sometimes there weren't. Sometimes there were parties; sometimes there weren't. Sometimes there was a short vacation somewhere; usually there wasn't.

With much of life so unpredictable and in flux, I grew to love the liturgical calendar of the church and that we could always count on its rhythm of Advent, Lent, Ordinary Time, and so on. It became a trusted and reliable friend.

I especially loved the season of Advent. As the somber companion of Christmas, I identified more with Advent's hymns in minor keys and its refusal to give up hope during a time of waiting. Christmas, with its holly, jolly music, tinsel, and an emphasis on consumerism in which I could not always partake, did not resonate with me quite as deeply as the rich beauty of Advent.

Advent is not the only reason I became ordained as a minister, but it is one of those uniquely "churchy" things that helps me love this call to ministry. Each Advent season brings with it the same four Sundays of candle lighting, contemplation, and hope in the midst of waiting. But it is also a time pregnant with possibility. Each Advent season calls us to a deeper understanding of our faith and of God. Each Advent season opens up new ways to understand and engage our world. And so it was for me, particularly in 2012 and 2013.

One of our lectionary texts for Advent is this passage from Luke 1:39-56. Luke begins his Gospel with the story of two very different pregnancies. Earlier in chapter 1 we meet Elizabeth and her husband, Zechariah, both of whom are righteous before God and both of whom have long waited to have a child. But according to the Bible, they are "getting on in years," and they haven't been able to conceive. Now, later in life, they have received the surprising and miraculous news that Elizabeth is pregnant. And then comes Mary, a young, unwed teenager who receives the shocking news that she, too, is with child. And this passage in Luke tells us what unfolds when these two women (who are cousins) meet.

> In those days Mary set out and went with haste to a Judean town in the hill country, where she entered the house of Zechariah and greeted Elizabeth. When Elizabeth heard Mary's greeting, the child leaped in her womb. And Elizabeth was filled with the Holy Spirit and exclaimed with a loud cry, "Blessed are you among women, and blessed is the fruit of your womb. And why has this happened to me, that the mother of my Lord comes to me? For as soon as I heard the sound of your greeting, the child in my womb leaped for joy. And blessed is she who believed that there would be a fulfillment of what was spoken to her by the Lord."
>
> And Mary said, "My soul magnifies the Lord, and my spirit rejoices in God my Savior, for he has looked with favor on the lowliness of his servant. Surely, from now on all generations will call me blessed; for the Mighty One has done great things for me, and holy is his name. His mercy is for those who fear him from generation to generation. He has shown strength with his arm; he has scattered the proud in the thoughts of their hearts. He has brought down the powerful from their thrones, and lifted up the lowly; he has filled the hungry with good things, and sent the rich away empty. He has helped his servant Israel, in remembrance of his mercy, according to the promise he made to our ancestors, to Abraham and to his descendants forever." And Mary remained with her about three months and then returned to her home. (Luke 1:39-56, NRSV)

While no two pregnancies are the same, each pregnancy is a time fraught with expectation and emotions. Joy and hope are certainly high on that list. But if we're honest, pregnancy is also filled with a good amount of fear and trembling.

Most expectant mothers I speak with begin the conversation with all that they are excited about—the delight, the anticipation, their hopes and dreams. But if you sit with these expectant mothers long enough, the conversation eventually circles around to their deeply held anxieties and uncertainties with what is to come. Concerns about the health of the baby, of the mother's own health, the health of relationships once the baby arrives, how siblings or pets might respond, any complications that might arise during second or third trimester or in the course of labor and delivery—all these fears lie within those who are expectant.

In the Advent of 2013, I was seven months pregnant. And I was intimately familiar with the gamut of emotions and mild waves of panic that inevitably wash over expectant parents, making us pause and wonder, "Can any of us ever really be ready to become stewards of another human life?" Carrying my own first son in my womb, I connected with this story of two pregnancies in a whole new way. I joined these two women, also expectant with their first sons, in their anticipation and uncertainty, in their joy and wonder.

And I felt for young Mary, hearing the news of a pregnancy she did not plan, a pregnancy that would not sit well with her parents or her community, a pregnancy that Joseph, her fiancé, did not yet know about. I imagined her fear and concern, the stress she must have been undergoing. After all, what would her parents say? How would her neighbors react? Would Joseph break off the engagement? Would she be left alone?

In the verses immediately preceding the lectionary text, Mary seemed to take the news from the angel fairly well, considering how huge the news actually was. But then, I think we get a sense of Mary's true state of mind in the first verse of today's story: "In those days Mary set out and went with haste to a Judean town in the hill country...." She "set out and *went with haste*"; in other words, she left town. In fact, she ran as fast as her first-trimester body would allow, seeking out her cousin Elizabeth, who she'd heard was also pregnant.

Who knows all the thoughts that flooded Mary's mind as she made that journey? Was she scared? Did she cry along the way—or laugh at the absurdity of it all? Did she rehearse how she might break the news to her family or to Joseph? Was she afraid and lost? Confused and overwhelmed? We can only use our holy imagination and wonder.

When Mary finally reached her destination and stood on Elizabeth's doorstep, I wonder if she had second thoughts about making her presence known. After all, how would her righteous cousin Elizabeth and Elizabeth's priestly husband respond to her premarital pregnancy? Would they believe her and take her in, or would they shame and shun her, turning her away? But with nowhere else to go, Mary takes a risk and greets her cousin.

Elizabeth's effusive response draws Mary in. In the midst of Mary's uncertainty and fear, Elizabeth envelops her in welcome and joy, without judgment or shame, accepting her and her situation, even blessing Mary and rejoicing with her.

We need more people like Elizabeth in this world, people whose joy for us can cut through our fear and doubt, people who put aside any impending judgment and offer God's love and grace to us. We need people who look at the world and see God's redeeming work at hand rather than seeing the worst in others and themselves. We need people like Elizabeth who can move us from a place of fear to a place of hope and singing. We need people like Elizabeth—people who see us, and can spot the expectant Christ child who longs to be born in us and in our lives.

Meister Eckhart, a German theologian and mystic, wrote long ago, "We are all called to be mothers of God, for God is always waiting to be born." For me, the Advent season of 2013 was particularly special as I wondered at the new life growing inside of me. There was something profound about being so expectant during a time when the church universal awaits a baby, and especially that year, when pregnant women actually made their way into the lectionary.

But then I think of Advents past and of Advents to come, and I am reminded that each one is profoundly special in its own way.

The previous year, in the Advent of 2012, I was not seven months pregnant. In fact, if there is a state that is the very opposite of pregnant, that's where I was. We had recently lost our first pregnancy to a miscarriage. And that season of Advent, singing those minor-key hymns and songs of longing and hope helped me to mourn that loss in a very distinct and necessary way. Furthermore, the fact that I was joined by a community of people that was also awaiting a child—not necessarily their own child who would join their family but the Christ child—brought great comfort to me. I realized that I was not alone. Rather, we were all waiting.

Advent has accompanied me through many important seasons of my life. Whether as one who grieved the loss of a pregnancy in 2012 or one who celebrated the continued growth of a healthy baby in 2013, Advent was there with me.

I think of my grandmother's last Advent season with us many years ago. She died in February, but was declining quickly through the weeks of December. And I remember how meaningful it was to await new life through the birth of a babe born in Bethlehem as my family walked with Grandmother through her end of life. She found so much hope and strength in the promises of the coming Christ child.

Advent is a season for all of us, and it holds profound depth and meaning for each of us, no matter where we are in life. Whether we are mourning loss, facing end of life, expecting first children or fifth grandchildren; whether we are enjoying a break from school or are burdened by the busyness of this season, Advent calls to us to pause and remember that "We are all called to be mothers of God, for God is always waiting to be born."

We are all bearers of God to this world, and the season of Advent is a time to remember that we are all called to be expectant, to be waiting and making preparations for Emmanuel, God with us. We need this season of Advent to prepare and make way, for what awaits us on the other side is completely and utterly life-changing. Those serene, silent-night nativity scenes do not do full justice to what God is bringing into the world through this child—just as sweet, cherubic pictures of sleeping babies do not do full justice to what new parents experience once their baby arrives.

This biblical story of two modest, pregnant women, Elizabeth and Mary, carrying the messenger and the Message, on the brink of changing the course of human history through what grows within them, shows us a glimpse of a world about to turn. It is the world that Mary sang of in her song, the song we've come to know as the Magnificat. "My soul magnifies the Lord," she sang. And she sang not just because of the good things God had done for her or me or you personally, but because of how the world was about to change.

Mary's song tells of a world in which the proud are scattered, the powerful are brought down, and the lowly are lifted up; of a world where the hungry are filled and the rich are sent away empty; a world where God hears and answers the cries of the lost, the last, the least, and the lonely. And a new world order is established where indeed the last shall be first and the first shall be last. Year after year, Mary's song is a radical one.

It is a song of hope birthed in a time of hopelessness and a song of joy birthed in a time of uncertainty. It is a time not so unlike our own: where disparities between the rich and the poor seem ever-more insurmountable; where there are those who feast until they are grossly full while others go away hungry; where some reside in homes filled with prettily packaged gifts while others have no place to call home at all.

It is into this time that Mary continues to sing and to dream of a different world. Through her song, she not only names those promises of God, but she is able to enter into them. She is able to claim her place in how the world might change. Songs are like that sometimes. They help us to believe the words we sing in ways we might not otherwise.

Mary sings, and in the season of Advent, we join her song, claiming our own place in how the world might change. Her song helps us to see how we are lodged in that promise. Her song helps us to recognize that we, too, give birth to Christ in this world through our actions and our lives and that we, too, can allow God to enter in, embodied in flesh, to become a real presence that brings about change.

There is risk, however, in that time of expectation, and there is risk in birth. We cannot live lives of complacency and comfort and expect new life to come unaided. We must take a dangerous journey, even as we are expectant, and we must sing and live transformation boldly. We do this because our Advent preparation and waiting is not just for the birth of a child, but also for the birth of a whole new way of life. It is a revolution, not fought with weapons of war, but with love, forgiveness, mercy, and healing. It is a revolution, brought not by force and powerful men, but by two pregnant women and the birth of a baby in a manger.

Madeleine L'Engle reminds us that there is no good time for birth to take place, "yet Love still takes the risk of birth." In each season of Advent, may we prepare our hearts and homes to be ready for Love to be born among and within us. Let us be expectant and allow hope to take root in us, so that come Christmas, we may know how to nurture that hope to blossom and flourish in our lives and in our world.

11

Discerning Kairos

YENA K. HWANG

For everything there is a season, and a time for every matter under heaven:

a time to be born and a time to die;
a time to plant, and a time to pluck up what is planted;
a time to kill, and a time to heal;
a time to break down, and a time to build up;
a time to weep, and a time to laugh;
a time to mourn, and a time to dance;
a time to throw away stones, and a time to gather stones together;
a time to embrace, and a time to refrain from embracing;
a time to seek, and a time to lose;
a time to keep, and a time to throw away;
a time to tear, and a time to sew;
a time to keep silence, and a time to speak;
a time to love and a time to hate;
a time for war, and a time for peace.

What gain have the workers from their toil? I have seen the business that God has given to everyone to be busy with. God has made everything suitable for its time. . . . I know that whatever God does endures forever; nothing can be added to it, nor anything taken from it; God has done this, so that all should stand in awe before [God]. (Ecclesiastes 3:1-11,14, NRSV)

There's an ancient Chinese saying that is neither ancient nor Chinese: "May you live in interesting times." You probably have heard many different terms describing this very "interesting" time we are in. Phyllis Tickle, in her book *The Great Emergence*, notes a pattern in Judeo-Christian history in which a period of stability and growth lasting about five hundred years is followed by a period of massive upheaval and change.[1] Lucky for us, the five-hundred-year period of stability is up, and we are living through another massive upheaval, where everything is changing, being questioned, reevaluated, and reformed.

Sure, reformation is a good thing! And we will be rewarded with another five hundred years of growth and prosperity. But first we have to endure a period of challenging struggles, uncertainty, and anxiety, which is the part that's not so fun. Tickle uses the term "emerging" to describe this time in which we, the church, are trying to figure out what to keep and what to throw away from our theological attic, so that we can reemerge—renewed.

Michael Jinkins, president of Louisville Seminary, defines the current time to be a similar "axial" age, an "exceptional historical moment" especially for Protestants. Mid-twentieth century philosopher Karl Jaspers coined the term "axial." Jaspers identified the historical era between 800 and 200 BCE as an axial age, an age in which teachers and philosophers such as Confucius and Lao-Tzu of China, Buddha of India, Zarathustra in Persia (present-day Iran), Plato in Greece, and Hebrew prophets in Palestine were on the world's stage, influencing and launching humanity forward.[2] According to Jaspers, "The intellectual and spiritual history of humanity . . . turned around this axial age; and as it turned, the whole world of humanity was unsettled by the turning."[3]

Whether we label it as an emerging time, an axial time, a hinge time, a transitional time, or an interesting time, many people would agree that the present is a difficult time to be the church. Yet, we have been called to be a church and serve the church "at such a time as this" (Esther 4:14), and we need some help in our process of discernment during this time of upheaval. There are many things to learn and unlearn, to review and analyze, and to which to apply our best critical thinking. We must adjust, but it isn't easy. It is hard to unlearn what we have learned. It is difficult to let go—oh, all the wonderful memories! Why do we have to deal with so many changes when the God we worship is immutable, unchanging? Does God even approve of all this change?

Since I lack the wisdom necessary to deal with life's big questions, I went seeking answers and ended up in the book of Ecclesiastes, the very source of wisdom. And I was pleased to learn that this beloved book was a source of some controversy in the first century CE, a controversy that lasted three hundred years. Known as the "Council of Jamnia," the rabbinic academy in Jamnia was called to settle the issue of finalizing the Hebrew canon (90 CE).[4] At this council, Ecclesiastes caused quite a debate between two schools of thoughts. One group argued that Ecclesiastes was too radical, bordering on heretical, to be included in the canon. The other group argued that it was an "inspired" text that needed to be included in the canon.[5] By the end of the first century, Ecclesiastes received the majority vote needed to be included in the Hebrew canon, but the controversy and disagreement persisted into the fourth century. I found this bit of history fascinating, comforting, and relevant to what we are experiencing, two thousand years after the Council of Jamnia. The content of our debates/disagreements has changed, but the fact that we debate over our disagreements is as old as time itself.

We are no strangers to disagreements and debates. In the Presbyterian Church (USA) alone we have seen many years of disagreements over particular issues that resulted in a division of our denomination. At the National Capital Presbytery, located near the nation's capital, we experience disagreements in various ways, being located near the nation's capital. However deeply polarized we may be as a nation, we know that we will continue to be one nation. However, when the polarization in our denomination led to a real separation in January of 2011, that reality impacted me more than I had expected. The separation created the Covenant Order of Evangelical Presbyterians, and we are still feeling the impact of their departure from the PC(USA). This process began when I was very involved at the presbytery level and the national level, which perhaps is another reason why I felt so disturbed by it. I struggled with the changes happening at the denominational level. I couldn't make sense of what it means to be one body of Christ with a group that chose to separate itself over differing theological views on who is welcome in the church universal.

As I struggled, I heard the message of Qohelet, the author of Ecclesiastes.[6] In the Septuagint (the Greek translation of the Old Testament) two different words are used to denote time: *kairos* and *chronos*. *Kairos* refers to appointed times and seasons, while *chronos* refers to a chronological time. When Qohelet speaks of time for "every matter" under heaven, that time is *kairos*, an appropriate time that is different than the chronological movement of time. Qohelet is stating that the author of those activities is God, not human beings. We are not in control; God is. We cannot manipulate the Holy Spirit to bring us to *kairos*. We forget this simple truth and go frantic trying to control everything that cannot be controlled, trying to usher in *kairos* when it is not ours to usher in. We want *kairos* to break through the *chronos* of current chaos to help us through this painful process, so that we can get to the healing, laughing, dancing, and embracing. *Can't we get there more quickly?* we wonder.

Maybe it's because we are Americans. We live in a place and time in which the miracle of modern medicine allows us to manipulate and choose even "a time to be born and a time to die," where the high-tech gadgets make us feel like the world is at our fingertips. We fool ourselves into believing that we are in control. Old Testament scholar Choon-Leong

Seow reminds us, "People cannot actually choose a time of birthing or dying. . . . Indeed, people do not decide when to heal, weep, laugh, mourn, lose, love, hate, or be in war or peace. These are occasions in which people find themselves, and they can only respond to them. All that mortals can do in the face of these times is to be open to them."[7]

The Ecclesiastes passage is not saying that every event of our lives is predetermined, or that we are not responsible for our own choices and actions. Rather, it is reminding us to recognize God as the one in control and show reverence before God and trust God to lead us through this and any other times of life. It is time to believe and trust these words of Qohelet: "Whatever has happened has already happened, and whatever will happen has already happened," and God will take care of all those matters that are beyond our grasp (Ecclesiastes 3:15, Seow translation).

It is not an answer, but perhaps our attempt to find answers is also vanity of vanities.

If the Judeo-Christian culture goes through a major rummage sale every five hundred years, I go through a personal/private theological rummage sale about every three years. It is a tiresome and inconvenient process, as it involves an existential and spiritual crisis each time. I felt disheartened by our situation in the PC(USA), in our nation, all the heartbreaking losses from natural disasters and violent acts being reported day in and day out. I was venting to an elder who is one of my mentors. In response to my grumblings about the institutionalized faults and criticisms, this faithful elder simply stated, "I don't know what's right and what's wrong, but I know that I belong to Christ and I like belonging to the community of Jesus Christ."

With that, *kairos* broke in. I had been asking the wrong questions, and thus arriving at wrong answers. The question is not about who or what is right or wrong. History has shown time and time again that things that were considered wrong are revealed to be right, like Galileo's theory on the revolution of the earth around the sun; and things that were accepted as right, like slavery, are revealed as being absolutely wrong. Thus the question is "What is important?" Do you want to belong to this often misguided yet always striving-to-be-faithful community of Christ's followers? Do you believe that the God of love will take care of God's people? Do you believe that God works through barriers to bring God's will for us? The Scriptures testify yes.

In *kairos*, God created the universe, a universe so vast that we cannot ever fathom it in regular *chronos* time. In *kairos*, God created humans in God's image; in *chronos*, humanity created God in their own image. In *kairos*, God brought the Hebrew people to be God's own people. In *chronos*, people debated and argued and rebelled, but in *kairos*, God sent prophets and leaders to reach out to the rebellious bunch to bring them back to God. In *chronos*, the Roman Empire overpowered the people of God, but in *kairos*, God sent a servant leader who could not be overthrown by any human authority. In *chronos*, he was crucified, but in *kairos*, he was raised from the dead. In *chronos*, the world awaits his glorious return, but in *kairos*, he is here every day.

He is in the face of the stranger whom we fear, in the child abandoned in the freezing cold to die, in the teenager being bullied, in the heartbreaking picture of the two victims embracing inside a collapsed factory in Bangladesh, in the despairing survivor trying to heal from an unspeakable act of terror at a finish line in Boston, in the frustrated worker trying to deal with being furloughed, in the faces of folks picking up the pieces of their lives shredded by a tornado, in the wounded soldier coming back with more missing than a limb, in the geriatric patient whose memory is disappearing, in the immigrant day laborers trying not to lose hope, in that politician whom we cannot stand, in the visitor in our pew who looks questionable, in the insignificant and nameless person cutting you off during the morning rush-hour traffic, even in the familiar faces we love dearly, but take for granted. In *kairos*, your eyes will open and see Jesus. Do you want God's *kairos*-time to break in and open your eyes?

My prayer is that as you break the bread of life, as you drink the cup of salvation, you will allow God's spirit to fill you—to open you wide, so that *kairos* will break open your *chronos* and help you to see what God is doing all around you, through you, in you, to bring the message of God's creative love, redemptive power, and generative renewal to all people, so that we may become true instruments of justice and peace. Amen.

NOTES

1. Phyllis Tickle, *The Great Emergence: How Christianity Is Changing and Why* (Grand Rapids: Baker Books, 2008), 16.
2. Michael Jinkins, "Transforming the Mind in the Service of God: A Case of Theological Education," *Mosaic* (Spring/Summer 2011): 13.
3. Ibid.
4. Choon-Leong Seow, *Ecclesiastes: A New Translation with Introduction and Commentary*, Anchor Bible 18C (New York: Doubleday, 1997), 3–4.
5. Ibid.
6. Qohelet is the Hebrew name of the book that we know as "Ecclesiastes," and it is traditionally translated as "teacher" or "preacher."
7. Seow, *Ecclesiastes*, 171.

12

"words, words, words...and the Word"

YENA K. HWANG

Based on John 1:1-16

words, words, words...
words that assault—words that comfort (Isaiah 40)
words that abandon—words that nurture
words that build walls—words that tear down those walls
words that control—words that set us free
words that criticize—words that encourage
words that darken—words that illuminate
words that defeat—words that prevail
words that hide—words that reveal
words that kill—words that create and birth new life
words that nullify and stupefy—words that justify and sanctify
words that push away—words that embrace
words that scatter—words that gather
words that steal—words that restore

words, words, words...
embodied/embellished
written
thought out
spoken/hushed and never spoken
lived out

words that exist even in the sheer silence of absurdity,
words that stab the heart and squash the soul,
words of desire, passion, and love mingled
with words of anger, fear, and pain...
what will it be?
saving words of grace, peace, and hope?
authentic words that transform?
kind and gentle words that soften harsh and twisted hearts?
words, words, Word...

In the beginning, God created the heavens and the earth with words...spoken, PROCLAIMED! (Genesis 1)
In the beginning was the Word and the Word was with God and the Word was God...and the Word became flesh and lived among us... (John 1)
speaking
words that revealed the truth, the way, the life;
words that pierced the hearts of the powerful few,
but healed the hearts of the powerless;
words that condemned and judged the wrongdoings
while forgiving the wrongdoers;
words that were fiercely passionate,
yet gentle as the spring breeze;
words that gave new direction and purpose to the lost,
who didn't even know they were lost;
words that became bread for the hungry,
and springs of water gushing up to eternal
life to the thirsty;
words that gave a sense of belonging to the displaced
and challenged the well-placed;
words that mystified and stupefied the "wise"
but enlightened the unwise fools;
words that invited the marginal, included the excluded,
enlarged the circle, and made room in the tent...

words that aggravated and irritated and challenged
his contemporaries,
words that inspired and transformed the world,
words that crucified him!
words that still aggravate, irritate, and challenge us today.

What words are on your tongue?
What words will you think and speak?

Let them not be arrogant words that assault,
clever words that entice,
disguised words that deceive,
fearful words that freeze the imagination,
hateful words that hinder,
justified words that pronounce injustice,
righteous words that reject.

Let us remember the Word and his words in the Beatitudes...
blessed are the poor in spirit
blessed are those who mourn
blessed are the meek
blessed are those who hunger and thirst for righteousness
blessed are the merciful
blessed are the pure in heart
blessed are the peacemakers (Matthew 5)

And speak
words of conviction without the condemnation,
words of grace that gather us up,
words of hope that heal,
words of peace seasoned with patience,
words of acceptance that recognize the undeniably authentic
work of the Holy in this unholy world of ours,
words of substance,
words that matter, no matter what mess of a situation we find
ourselves in,
words that keep us connected, even through our difference.

The Word became flesh and lived among us.
The Word—Jesus Christ, his life, death, and resurrection—is our only guide, conscience, and standard of word spoken and embodied and lived out.
Now, give this sister a word!

Epilogue

Words for the Rest of Us

LAURA MARIKO CHEIFETZ

Some of my best friends are Korean American clergywomen. That isn't even a tongue-in-cheek insult. It's true.

I am not Korean American. I'm Asian Pacific American (although fourth-generation and biracial, of Japanese and white Jewish descent). I'm a woman. I'm an ordained minister.

Growing up, one of the best ways for me to make sense of my experience as a biracial person, a Japanese American, and someone coming from a Jewish family, was through other people's narratives: history, literature, movies, anything. They were not my stories, but they were stories that named truths—truths of my experience and truths I will never personally know. Stories taught me to broaden my perspectives, to learn more about other regions and other peoples.

This collection of narratives, reflections, and sermons makes me think about what I have in common with Korean American clergywomen, and what is very different about us. My family has been in the U.S. since the early 1900s, whereas most Koreans arrived post-1965, when immigration legislation was reformed and doors were opened for those coming from continents other than Europe. Much of the differences between Japanese Americans and Korean Americans stem from our very different histories and cultures, as well as from our distinct patterns of immigration. Korea has had high rates of emigration since 1965 while Japan's emigration slowed considerably with anti-Japanese legislation in the early twentieth century, and it has remained low over the years. Koreans endured brutal Japanese occupation, a war, the division of a nation and its families, and now long-term U.S. military presence. Through it all, the Korean church provided a narrative of liberation, a gospel of freedom and comfort, and a place that more and more Koreans and Korean Americans call home. Japanese Americans have been shaped by the internment of 120,000 Japanese nationals and Japanese American citizens during World War II. There are few Japanese churches left in the U.S.

Given the low numbers of Japanese American biracial women ministers, I have naturally migrated toward other Asian Pacific American women ministers. While we are no more special than anyone else, the ways in which we experience our life and work are distinct. Korean American women ministers have narratives that are specific to being Korean American and women. Their stories are not mine, but they remind me of the complexity of those churches that (sometimes accidentally) loved and nurtured and encouraged those of us who have been called to ministry. Many of our churches remain flawed and hurtful places.

In their particularity, we can't use these stories to generalize about Korean American clergywomen. We can use these stories to illuminate who we are. For me, they tell me a little more about being a clergywomen, about being part of the church that confirms the call God places on each of us and yet communicates to us that we aren't always enough, where sexism and racism and age-ism trump God.

The stories in this book are an important piece of what defines and shapes the North American church. These women write of being rejected, loved, discouraged, given opportunities, all in the context of the church. The church in all of its local expressions is capable of each of these reactions. I have joked before that the choice I face in choosing a church is whether I have a higher tolerance for theological conservatism (with its accompanying homophobia) or white liberal racism and uptight white worship. Most days, I choose the latter. Many of the writers in this book have chosen the former. And many do not get a choice.

Thanks to the ways in which our own churches treat us, Asian Pacific American women, but particularly Korean American women, face a different set of options: Serve in the Korean American church community and work through Confucianism confused with Christianity, or serve in the dominant culture church community and struggle with facing discrimination based on accent, culture, and race.

Mickie Choi says, "People need our flowers today." She tells us not to be stingy toward the people we have around us. These chapters are like flowers to the Korean American church, to women, to clergywomen, to the white dominant church. These words are acts of generosity, gifts of honest and loving wisdom.

Now that we have read these words, what do we do with them? Continuing on in the status quo, wherein sexism and racism are expected norms, traps all of us in a pattern in which we fall short of the witness to which God has called the church. Surely, we as a church are meant to be a place where flawed, broken human beings gather, and where we experience immense grace, mystery, beauty, and the flourishing of who we are called to be. A church that shames a woman minister on the occasion of her ordination is redeemed by a church that gathers to celebrate her call to ministry, but this community response does not excuse the initial reaction.

I realize I have come to expect several things out of most church gatherings. I expect that my age, my gender, my physical appearance, my ordained status, my reproductive status, and my racial background will come up in conversation. Someone is surprised I'm an ordained minister. Someone has to know whether I want to have kids. Someone inquires into my racial identity. Despite my increasingly salt-and-pepper hair, my (lower-than-average) age continues to be a topic of great interest. I do not appreciate the presumption that I should answer these questions or graciously respond to exclamations of surprise. But I'm not ashamed or embarrassed by my answers, because I do not think who I am is wrong.

Too often, Korean American clergywomen are told that who they are is wrong. They have an accent that is too immigrant-sounding, or they don't speak Korean. They are women. Some are not married, or if married, don't have children. They don't look like pastors. They are too young. Some are told they will struggle serving a dominant culture church because they grew up in a Korean church, while others who did not grow up in the Korean church are questioned about their level of Korean-ness. But they persist, because they know they are called. They know there is something greater than the worst reactions of their own Korean and the larger dominant culture church communities.

There is a Japanese word I would use here. It is *gaman*. Endure.

What I have learned about my Korean American clergywomen sisters and colleagues is that there are times when we as women of Asian Pacific descent endure, and there are times when we protest. There are times when we refuse to take one more micro-aggression as a given. We give ourselves permission to believe that God created us, just as God created each being in this universe.

The church does not have to be the place that tells us, or anyone, that who we are isn't quite right. Instead, the church can be the place where we come home to feel at rest, to be launched into ministry and mission. These words, like flowers, could cause the church to pause by them, breathe deeply their fragrance, and consider the world differently. We who serve the church, who have been a part of the church for as long as we can remember or as long as we have believed, can choose to make the church a very different place.

About the Contributors

Dr. Aram Bae received the Bachelor of Arts in Education and Child Study from Smith College, a Master of Divinity from Princeton Theological Seminary, a Master of Christian Education from Union Presbyterian Seminary, and her doctorate in Practical Theology from Union Theological Seminary. She is a candidate in the Presbyterian Church (USA) and is currently Director of Family Ministries at the Fifth Avenue Presbyterian Church in New York City. She is also adjunct professor at the New York Theological Seminary, teaching courses on faith and curriculum development.

Rev. Laura Mariko Cheifetz is a double-P.K. Presbyterian minister of Japanese and white Jewish descent, currently living in Louisville, Kentucky, and serving at the Presbyterian Publishing Corporation. A graduate of Western Washington University, McCormick Theological Seminary, and the North Park University School of Business and Non-Profit Management, Laura has worked with Asian American, Latino, and African American young adults and pastors, new pastors, and scholars in vocational formation, and in sharing about resources with the wider church. She enjoys her family, dinner parties with friends, and political television dramas, along with her two Shih Tzus.

Rev. Dr. Mickie Choi was born in Seoul, Korea, into a family of educators five days after the Korean War broke out. She graduated from Yonsei University. She did graduate studies at the University of Southern California and the University of the Pacific, Stockton, California, earning her Master of Science in Physical Chemistry and PhD in Pharmaceutical Chemistry. While she teaching chemistry at the University of Lavern, she felt strongly called by God to the ministry and obtained a Master of Divinity from International School of Theology. She received her Doctor of Ministry from San Francisco Theological Seminary. Now a teaching elder and member of the Presbytery of Riverside, California, she is working as Development Specialist/Regional Representative of the West Regional Office of the Presbyterian Church (USA) Investment and Loan Program, helping local congregations and governing bodies of PC (USA) to build churches.

Rev. Nayoung Ha is a teaching elder of the Presbyterian Church (USA) and a PhD candidate in Systematic Theology and Ethics at the Lutheran School of Theology at Chicago. Her specialized ministry as Organizing Director at Korean American Resource and Cultural Center is focused on immigrants' rights and advocacy work for low-income, marginalized, or/ and undocumented Korean American community. She has a Master of Divinity from Hanshin Graduate School of Theology, Seoul, South Korea, and a Master of Arts in Theological Studies from McCormick Theological Seminary. Her interests include the issues of domestic violence, identities and differences, human rights, and interfaith dialogue.

Rev. Dr. Christine J. Hong is Assistant Professor of Worship and Evangelism at Louisville Presbyterian Theological Seminary. Previously she was Associate for Theology: Interfaith Relations, in Theology and Worship, a ministry area of the Presbyterian Mission Agency. She is a teaching elder in the Presbyterian Church (USA) and has spent time in the pastorate as both a religious educator and young adult minister in New York and Southern California. Christine holds a PhD in Practical Theology from the Claremont School of Theology.

She also holds an MDiv and ThM from Princeton Theological Seminary. She has worked with New Vision Partners and the Center for Global Peacebuilding.

Rev. Yena K. Hwang is Associate Pastor for Christian Formation at Fairfax Presbyterian Church in Virginia. Yena received her Master of Divinity from Princeton Theological Seminary and a Master of Arts in Marriage and Family Therapy from Louisville Presbyterian Seminary. Yena is married to Rick Choi and has two sons, Justin and Nathan.

Rev. Dr. Grace Ji-Sun Kim received her Master of Divinity from Knox College (University of Toronto) and her PhD from the University of Toronto. She is Associate Professor of Theology at Earlham School of Religion. Kim is author of eight other books: *Embracing the Other* (Eerdmans), *Christian Doctrines for Global Gender Justice* coedited with Jenny Daggers (Palgrave Macmillan), *Theological Reflections on "Gangnam Style": A Racial, Sexual, and Cultural Critique* cowritten with Joseph Cheah, *Contemplations from the Heart* (Wipf & Stock), *Reimagining with Christian Doctrines* coedited with Jenny Daggers (Palgrave Macmillan), *Colonialism, Han and the Transformative Power* (Palgrave Macmillan), *The Holy Spirit, Chi and the Other* (Palgrave Macmillan), and *The Grace of Sophia* (Pilgrim Press). She is coeditor with Dr. Joseph Cheah of the Palgrave Macmillan book series, "Asian Christianity in Diaspora." Kim is a teaching elder in the Presbyterian Church (USA).

Rev. Jean Kim is a retired minister/staff of PC(USA) for the issue of homelessness. She is a Washington State certified social worker and mental health counselor. Jean is founder of several homeless missions, including the Church of Mary Magdalene and Korean Nest Mission. She has been serving homeless people for the past four decades and has received nineteen awards, including the Women of Faith Award from

PC(USA) and the Medal of Honor from the Korean government. Rev. Kim has authored several books on the issues of homelessness and women's leadership in the church. She has four degrees: two bachelor's in Theology and English literature, a Master of Social Work, and a Doctor of Ministry.

Rev. Mihee Kim-Kort is an ordained minister in the Presbyterian Church (USA). She earned her Master of Divinity and Master of Theology from Princeton Theological Seminary. She has published two books: *Making Paper Cranes: Toward an Asian American Feminist Theology* (Chalice Press), *Streams Run Uphill: Conversations with Young Clergywomen of Color* (Judson Press), and *Yoked: Stories of a Clergy Couple in Marriage, Family, and Ministry* (Rowman and Littlefield). Currently, she resides with her family in Bloomington, Indiana, where she leads a Presbyterian college ministry.

Rev. Joann Haejong Lee was ordained as a teaching elder in the Presbyterian Church (USA). She has served as a Lilly Pastoral Resident at Fourth Presbyterian Church in Chicago and as Associate Pastor at The House of Hope Presbyterian Church in Saint Paul and Calvary Presbyterian Church in San Francisco. She was born in New York City to Korean immigrant parents and grew up in Houston, Texas. She has a Master of Divinity from McCormick Theological Seminary, and a Bachelor of Arts in English and Psychology from the University of Texas, Austin. Joann and her spouse, Mike, met in eighth grade and now live in San Francisco with their two dogs, Bailey and Logan, and their first child, born in January 2014.

Rev. Dr. Unzu Lee was born in Korea, immigrated to Brazil at age fourteen, and then immigrated to the U.S. at age seventeen. She considers herself a 1.5 generation Asian American of Korean descent. Lee is a fifth-generation Christian who grew up in a Christian family that takes faith in action very seriously, and this led her to study theology and ministry at Princeton

Theological Seminary, Women's Theological Center, and Episcopal Divinity School. Lee was ordained as a teaching elder in the PC(USA) in 1995 and has served as Coordinator for Women's Advocacy and Presbyterian Women's associate for leadership. She was a PC(USA) delegate to the eighth assembly of the World Council of Churches, and in 2007–2010 she served on the Gender Justice Network of the World Association of Reformed Churches representing PC(USA). She coauthored *Searching for Home: Home Is Where Stories Are Told* (in Korean) and *Singing the Lord's Song in a New Land* (in English), and authored *Coming Home: Asian American Women Doing Theology* (English). She has served on the special committee of the National Council of Korea Presbyterian Churches, created to study the status of women in Korean immigrant churches, and has accompanied the journey of National Korean Presbyterian Women since 1995.

Rev. Irene Pak was born and raised in Ogden, Utah. She is a lifelong Presbyterian and graduated with her Master of Divinity at McCormick Theological Seminary. Pak served for four years as Associate Pastor of English Ministries and Christian Education at Daesung Korean Presbyterian Church in Sunnyvale, California, and currently serves as Associate Pastor at Stone Church of Willow Glen in San Jose, California. She loves to read, play music, cook, exercise, and eat good food.

Rev. Dr. Neal D. Presa is Associate Pastor of the 1,100-member Village Community Presbyterian Church in Rancho Santa Fe, California (villagechurch.org), and Extraordinary Associate Professor of Practical Theology with the North-West University in Potschefstroom, South Africa. He most recently served as moderator of the 220th General Assembly (2012) of the Presbyterian Church (USA), the third Asian American to have been elected to that post.